SIGNAL 2016

The First International Conference on Advances in Signal, Image and Video Processing

June 26 - 30, 2016

Lisbon, Portugal

SIGNAL 2016 Editors

Wilfried Uhring, ICube, University of Strasbourg and CNRS, France

Rafael Caldeirinha, Instituto de Telecomunicações | Polytechnic Institute of Leiria, Portugal

Constantin Paleologu, University Politehnica of Bucharest, Romania

Printed from e-media with permission by:

Curran Associates, Inc.
57 Morehouse Lane
Red Hook, NY 12571

Some format issues inherent in the e-media version may also appear in this print version.

Printed by Curran Associates, Inc. (2016)

International Academy, Research, and Industry Association (IARIA)
412 Derby Way
Wilmington, DE 19810

Phone: (408) 893-6407
Fax: (408) 527-6351

petre@iaria.org

Additional copies of this publication are available from:

Curran Associates, Inc.
57 Morehouse Lane
Red Hook, NY 12571 USA
Phone: 845-758-0400
Fax: 845-758-2633
Email: curran@proceedings.com
Web: www.proceedings.com

Table of Contents

SIGNAL 2016

Foreword

The First International Conference on Advances in Signal, Image and Video Processing (SIGNAL 2016), held between June 26 - 30, 2016 - Lisbon, Portugal, was an inaugural event. Signal, video and image processing constitutes the basis of communications systems. With the proliferation of portable/implantable devices, embedded signal processing became widely used, despite that most of the common users are not aware of this issue. New signal, image and video processing algorithms and methods, in the context of a growing-wide range of domains (communications, medicine, finance, education, etc.) have been proposed, developed and deployed. Moreover, since the implementation platforms experience an exponential growth in terms of their performance, many signal processing techniques are reconsidered and adapted in the framework of new applications. Having these motivations in mind, the goal of this conference was to bring together researchers and industry and form a forum for fruitful discussions, networking, and ideas.

We take here the opportunity to warmly thank all the members of the SIGNAL 2016 Technical Program Committee, as well as the numerous reviewers. The creation of such a high quality conference program would not have been possible without their involvement. We also kindly thank all the authors who dedicated much of their time and efforts to contribute to SIGNAL 2016. We truly believe that, thanks to all these efforts, the final conference program consisted of top quality contributions.

Also, this event could not have been a reality without the support of many individuals, organizations, and sponsors. We are grateful to the members of the SIGNAL 2016 organizing committee for their help in handling the logistics and for their work to make this professional meeting a success.

We hope that SIGNAL 2016 was a successful international forum for the exchange of ideas and results between academia and industry and for the promotion of progress in the field of signal processing.

We are convinced that the participants found the event useful and communications very open. We also hope that Lisbon provided a pleasant environment during the conference and everyone saved some time for exploring this beautiful city.

SIGNAL 2016 Chairs:

Constantin Paleologu, University Politehnica of Bucharest, Romania
Wilfried Uhring, ICube, University of Strasbourg and CNRS, France
Malka N. Halgamuge, University of Melbourne, Australia
Sergey Yurish, Excelera, S. L. | IFSA, Spain
Rafael Caldeirinha, Instituto de Telecomunicações | Polytechnic Institute of Leiria, Portugal
Nicolas H. Younan, Mississippi State University, USA
Ramesh Rayudu, Victoria University of Wellington, New Zealand

SIGNAL 2016

Committee

SIGNAL 2016 Advisory Committee

Constantin Paleologu, University Politehnica of Bucharest, Romania
Wilfried Uhring, ICube, University of Strasbourg and CNRS, France
Malka N. Halgamuge, University of Melbourne, Australia
Sergey Yurish, Excelera, S. L. | IFSA, Spain
Rafael Caldeirinha, Instituto de Telecomunicações | Polytechnic Institute of Leiria, Portugal
Nicolas H. Younan, Mississippi State University, USA
Ramesh Rayudu, Victoria University of Wellington, New Zealand

SIGNAL 2016 Technical Program Committee

Andrea F. Abate, University of Salerno, Italy
Aydin Akan, Istanbul University & Izmir Katip Celebi University, Turkey
Zahid Akhtar, University of Udine, Italy
Felix Albu, Valahia University of Targoviste, Romania
Kiril Alexiev, Institute for Information and Communication Technologies - Bulgarian Academy of Sciences, Bulgaria
Cristian Anghel, University Politehnica of Bucharest, Romania
Ognjen Arandjelović, University of St Andrews, Scotland, UK
João Ascenso, Instituto Superior Técnico - Instituto de Telecomunicações (IT), Portugal
Pedro Assuncao, Instituto de Telecomunicacoes / IPLeiria, Portugal
Lutfiye Durak Ata, Istanbul Technical University | Informatics Institute, Turkey
Nadia Baaziz, Université du Québec en Outaouais, Canada
Vesh Raj Sharma Banjade, Intel Corporation, USA
Aryaz Baradarani, Institute for Diagnostic Imaging Research (IDIR) - University of Windsor, Canada
Sofia Ben Jebara, Ecole Supérieure des Communications de Tunis, Tunisia
Wassim Ben Chikha, Tunisia Polytechnic School | Carthage University, Tunisia
Stefano Berretti, University of Florence, Italy
Silvia Biasotti, Consiglio Nazionale delle Ricerche - Istituto di Matematica Applicata e Tecnologie Informatiche 'E. Magenes', Genoa, Italy
Jacques Blanc-Talon, DGA, France
Leonardo Bocchi, University of Florence, Italy
Miguel Bordallo, University of Oulu, Finland
Radoslav Bortel, Czech Technical University in Prague, Czech Republic
Abdel-Ouahab Boudraa, Ecole Navale/Arts & Métiers ParisTech, France
Xavier Briottet, The French Aeropace Lab ONERA, France
Rafael Caldeirinha, Instituto de Telecomunicações | Polytechnic Institute of Leiria, Portugal
Roberto Caldelli, CNIT - National Interuniversity Consortium for Telecommunications, Florence, Italy
Jaime S. Cardoso, INESC TEC & University of Porto, Portugal
George Caridakis, National Technical University of Athens, Greece
Pierre Chainais, Univ. Lille | UMR 9189 - CRIStAL - Centre de Recherche en Informatique, FranceChin-Chen Chang, Feng Chia University, Taiwan

Jocelyn Chanussot, Grenoble Institute of Technology, France
Amitava Chatterjee, Jadavpur University, India
Dmitry Chetverikov, Eötvös Loránd University (ELTE) / Institute for Computer Science and Control (MTA SZTAKI), Hungary
Doru Florin Chiper, Technical University Gheorghe Asachi Iasi, Romania
Ryszard S. Choras, University of Technology & Life Sciences, Poland
Silviu Ciochina, University Politehnica of Bucharest, Romania
Cristian Contan, Technical University of Cluj-Napoca, Romania
Francois Xavier Coudoux, Université de Valenciennes et du Hainaut-Cambrésis, France
Matthew Davies, INESC TEC, Porto, Portugal
Philippe Delachartre, Université de Lyon, France
António Dourado, University of Coimbra, Portugal
Fadoua Drira, University of Sfax, Tunisia
Simina Emerich, Technical University of Cluj-Napoca, Romania
Youssef Fakhri , Faculty of Sciences - Ibn Tofail University, Morocco
Ranran Feng, University of Texas at Dallas, USA
Germain Forestier, University of Haute-Alsace, France
Said Gaci, Sonatrach, Algeria
Víctor P. Gil, Universidad Carlos III de Madrid, Spain
Jerome Gilles, San Diego State University, USA
Gaetano Giunta, University of "Roma TRE", Italy
Elena González, Universidade de Vigo, Spain
Irene Y. H. Gu, Chalmers University of Technology, Gothenburg, Sweden
Pietro Guccione, Politecnico di Bari, Italy
Malka N. Halgamuge, University of Melbourne, Australia
Wassim Hamidouche, INSA de Rennes / IETR, France
Paul Honeine, University of Rouen, France
Pengyu Hong, Brandeis University, USA
Izumi Ito, Tokyo Institute of Technology, Japan
Edouard Ivanjko, University of Zagreb, Croatia
Yuji Iwahori, Chubu University, Japan
Rachid Jennane, Université d'Orléans - Polytech'Orléans, France
Li-Wei Kang, National Yunlin University of Science and Technology, Taiwan
Sokratis K. Katsikas, Gjøvik University College, Norway
Drossos Konstantinos, Tampere University of Technology, Finland
Konstantinos Koutroumbas, Institute for Space Applications and Remote Sensing - National Observatory of Athens, Greece
Jaroslaw Kozlak, AGH University of Science and Technology, Poland
Andrea Kutics, International Christian University, Japan
Marco Leo, National Research Council of Italy - Institute of Applied Sciences and Intelligent Systems, Italy
Chunshu Li, IMEC, Leuven, Belgium
Tatjana Loncar-Turukalo, University of Novi Sad, Serbia
Pavel Loskot, Swansea University, UK
Sylvain Marchand, University of La Rochelle, France
Jorge Manuel Miranda Dias, Khalifa University of Science, Technology & Research (KUSTAR), Abu Dhabi, UAE
El Mustapha Mouaddib, University of Picardie Jules Verne, France

Jian Yu, Auckland University of Technology, New Zealand
Sergey Yurish, Excelera, S. L. | IFSA, Spain
Zhongyuan Zhao, Beijing University of Posts and Telecommunications, China
Catalin Zorila, Toshiba Cambridge Research Laboratory, UK

Copyright Information

For your reference, this is the text governing the copyright release for material published by IARIA.

The copyright release is a transfer of publication rights, which allows IARIA and its partners to drive the dissemination of the published material. This allows IARIA to give articles increased visibility via distribution, inclusion in libraries, and arrangements for submission to indexes.

I, the undersigned, declare that the article is original, and that I represent the authors of this article in the copyright release matters. If this work has been done as work-for-hire, I have obtained all necessary clearances to execute a copyright release. I hereby irrevocably transfer exclusive copyright for this material to IARIA. I give IARIA permission or reproduce the work in any media format such as, but not limited to, print, digital, or electronic. I give IARIA permission to distribute the materials without restriction to any institutions or individuals. I give IARIA permission to submit the work for inclusion in article repositories as IARIA sees fit.

I, the undersigned, declare that to the best of my knowledge, the article is does not contain libelous or otherwise unlawful contents or invading the right of privacy or infringing on a proprietary right.

Following the copyright release, any circulated version of the article must bear the copyright notice and any header and footer information that IARIA applies to the published article.

IARIA grants royalty-free permission to the authors to disseminate the work, under the above provisions, for any academic, commercial, or industrial use. IARIA grants royalty-free permission to any individuals or institutions to make the article available electronically, online, or in print.

IARIA acknowledges that rights to any algorithm, process, procedure, apparatus, or articles of manufacture remain with the authors and their employers.

I, the undersigned, understand that IARIA will not be liable, in contract, tort (including, without limitation, negligence), pre-contract or other representations (other than fraudulent misrepresentations) or otherwise in connection with the publication of my work.

Exception to the above is made for work-for-hire performed while employed by the government. In that case, copyright to the material remains with the said government. The rightful owners (authors and government entity) grant unlimited and unrestricted permission to IARIA, IARIA's contractors, and IARIA's partners to further distribute the work.

Super-resolving a Single Blurry Image Through Blind Deblurring Using ADMM

Xiangrong Zeng, Yan Liu, Jun Fan, Qizi Huangpeng, Jing Feng, Jinlun Zhou, Maojun Zhang

College of Information System and Management
National University of Defense Technology
Changsha, China 410073
Email: zengxrong@gmail.com

***Abstract*—Both single blind image super-resolution (SBISR) and blind image deblurring (BID) are ill-posed inverse problems typically addressed by imposing some form of regularization (prior knowledge) on the unknown blurs and original images (the high resolution image and the sharp image for SBISR and BID, respectively). However, SBISR is more ill-posed than BID due to the introduce of the downsampling operator in the former, thus, the latter is usually easier to be solved than the former. We propose to address the SBISR problem by a BID method via reformulating it into a BID problem by an interpolation operator, and then solving the BID problem using the alternating direction method of multipliers (ADMM). Our approach bridges the gap between SBISR and BID, taking advantages of existing BID methods to handle SBISR. Experiments on synthetic and real blurry images (also on a real sharp image) show that the proposed method is effective, and competitive in terms of speed and restoration quality.**

Keywords–Image super-resolution; Blind image deblurring; ADMM.

I. Introduction

Single image super-resolution (SISR)[1-8] aims at recovering a high-resolution (HR) image $\mathbf{x} \in \mathbb{R}^{N_h}$ from a low-resolution (LR) input image $\mathbf{y} \in \mathbb{R}^{N_l}$ which is defined to be the LR noisy version of the HR image as

$$\mathbf{y} = \mathbf{DBx} + \mathbf{n} \tag{1}$$

where $\mathbf{D} : \mathbb{R}^{N_h} \rightarrow \mathbb{R}^{N_l} (N_l < N_h)$ is the downsampling matrix, $\mathbf{B} : \mathbb{R}^{N_h} \rightarrow \mathbb{R}^{N_h}$ is the blurring matrix, and $\mathbf{n} \in \mathbb{R}^{N_l}$ is the additive noise term. The SISR problem is typically severely ill-posed since $\mathbf{DB}$ is rectangular with more columns than rows, and it is more ill-posed than *multi-frame super-resolution* (MFSR) [9][10] and, thus, it can only be solved satisfactorily via regularization by utilizing an image model or prior. If $\mathbf{B}$ is the identity, then (1) reduces to the image interpolation problem [11][12] under noise; if $\mathbf{B}$ is unknown, then (1) evolves to *single blind image super-resolution* (SBISR), which is more complicated than the SISR one and more realistic, and is the focus of this paper. However, most SISR methods assume that $\mathbf{B}$ is known, that is, it is usually predefined, such as Gaussian blur [13], bicubic interpolation [7][8], Gaussian blur followed by bicubic interpolation [14], simple pixel averaging [2], and so on. Only a few works have been dedicated to the SBISR problem. For instance, a parametric Gaussian model with unknown width was assumed for the blur kernel in [13][15][16], and its extension to multiple parametric models was proposed in [17]. A nonparametric model for kernel recovery was presented in [18] via assuming that the kernel has a single peak. All these methods have a restrictive assumption on the blur kernel.

Recently, [19] showed that an accurate blur model is critical to the success of SISR algorithms, and [20] presented that the PSF of the camera is the wrong blur kernel to use in SISR algorithms, and showed how to correct the blur kernel from the LR image. Both [19] and [20] seek accurate blur kernels based on existing SISR algorithms (such as [6][7][8] with complex nature and costly computation), and, thus, their complexities are even more than those of the SISR ones.

In this paper, we address the SBISR problem via a *blind image deblurring* (BID) method, and the rationale behind this idea is that BID is usually easier to be solved than SBISR. The proposed method first reformulates the SBISR problem into a BID one by an interpolation operator, and then handle the BID by alternating minimization, in which, each sub-problem is efficiently solved by the *alternating direction method of multipliers* (ADMM) [21][22]. Thus, the proposed method bridges the gap between SBISR and BID, benefitting from that some BID methods (such as [23-27] and many others omitted here due to space limiation) are arguably faster and easier to understand, than state-of-the-art SISR/SBISR methods, and reaching competitive speed and restoration quality. The paper is organized as follows: Section II introduces the proposed approach, Section III reports experimental results, and Section IV ends the paper with the conclusion.

II. Proposed Approach

This section introduces how to reformulate a SBISR problem into a BID one and how to solve the resulting BID problem.

A. Problem formulation

Based on the notations in (1), we first introduce the BID problem, which aims at estimating an image $\mathbf{x}$ from a single observed blurry image $\mathbf{z} \in \mathbb{R}^{N_h}$ satisfying a convolutional degradation model

$$\mathbf{z} = \mathbf{Bx} + \mathbf{s} \tag{2}$$

where $\mathbf{s} \in \mathbb{R}^{N_h}$ is the additive noise. BID is also a severely ill-posed problem since the image $\mathbf{x}$, the blurring matrix $\mathbf{B}$ and the noise $\mathbf{s}$ are all unknown. In order to build the relationship between the problems of BID and SBISR, inserting (2) into (1) yields

$$\mathbf{y} = \mathbf{D}(\mathbf{z} - \mathbf{s}) + \mathbf{n} = \mathbf{Dz} + (\mathbf{n} - \mathbf{Ds}) \tag{3}$$

which indicates that the SBISR is more ill-posed than the BID, since both aim to recover $\mathbf{x}$ from $\mathbf{y}$ and $\mathbf{z}$, respectively, with unknown $\mathbf{B}$, but the former has fewer known samples than the latter due to the introduce of $\mathbf{D}$ (namely, the length of $\mathbf{y}$ is less than that of $\mathbf{z}$). This inspires that we can solve the SBISR problem in an easier way via reformulating it into a BID problem. The idea is to first interpolate the LR image $\mathbf{y}$ as

$$\mathbf{u} = \mathbf{U}\mathbf{y} = \mathbf{U}\mathbf{D}\mathbf{B}\mathbf{x} + \mathbf{U}\mathbf{n} \tag{4}$$

where $\mathbf{U}$ is the interpolation operator (for instance, the *bicubic* or *bilinear* interpolation operators, or other advanced interpolation operators [11][12]), $\mathbf{u} \in \mathbb{R}^{N_h}$ is the interpolation of $\mathbf{y}$. Then we can rewrite (4) as

$$\mathbf{u} = \mathbf{K}\mathbf{x} + \mathbf{e} = \mathbf{X}\mathbf{k} + \mathbf{e} \tag{5}$$

where $\mathbf{K} = \mathbf{U}\mathbf{D}\mathbf{B} \in \mathbb{R}^{N_h} \times \mathbb{R}^{N_h}$ is the new blurring matrix corresponding to a blur filter $\mathbf{k} \in \mathbb{R}^{N_h}$, and $\mathbf{X} \in \mathbb{R}^{N_h} \times \mathbb{R}^{N_h}$ is the square matrix representing the convolution of image $\mathbf{x}$ with the filter $\mathbf{k}$, and $\mathbf{e} = \mathbf{U}\mathbf{n}$ is the interpolation of $\mathbf{n}$.

Thus, instead of super-resolving $\mathbf{x}$ from $\mathbf{y}$ (see (1)), the HR image can be obtained via bind deblurring of $\mathbf{x}$ from $\mathbf{u}$ (see (5), which becomes the new focus of this paper):

$$(\hat{\mathbf{x}}, \hat{\mathbf{k}}) = \arg\min_{\mathbf{x},\mathbf{k}} \tfrac{\lambda}{2}\|\mathbf{K}\mathbf{x} - \mathbf{u}\|_2^2 + \phi_{\text{GTV}}(\mathbf{x}) + \iota_{\mathcal{S}}(\mathbf{k}) \tag{6}$$

where λ is a positive parameter, ϕ_{GTV} a *generalized total variation* (GTV) regularizer given by

$$\phi_{\text{GTV}}(\mathbf{x}) = \|\mathbf{D}_h\mathbf{x}\|_p^p + \|\mathbf{D}_v\mathbf{x}\|_p^p = \sum_i |[\mathbf{D}_h\mathbf{x}]_i|^p + |[\mathbf{D}_v\mathbf{x}]_i|^p$$

where $\mathbf{D}_h$ and $\mathbf{D}_v$ denote the horizontal and vertical derivative partial operator, respectively. Since the distribution of gradients of natural images is more heavy-tailed than Laplace distribution (see [28]), we set $0 \le p \le 1$. $\iota_{\mathcal{S}}$ is the indicator function of the set $\mathcal{S}$ which is the probability simplex

$$\mathcal{S} = \{\mathbf{k} : \mathbf{k} \succeq 0, \|\mathbf{k}\|_1 = 1\}. \tag{7}$$

B. Proposed algorithm framework

Alternatively minimizing (6) with respect to $\mathbf{x}$ and $\mathbf{k}$, while increasing the parameter λ, yields the following framework:

Algorithm *Proposed algorithmic framework*

1. **Input**: Observed LR image $\mathbf{y}$, λ and $\alpha > 1$.
2. **Step I**: Interpolate $\mathbf{y}$ via $\mathbf{u} = \mathbf{U}\mathbf{y}$.
3. **Step II**: Blind estimation of blur filter $\mathbf{k}$ from $\mathbf{u}$, by alternative loop over coarse-to-fine levels:
4. ► Update the image estimate

$$\hat{\mathbf{x}} \leftarrow \arg\min_{\mathbf{x}} \tfrac{\lambda}{2}\|\hat{\mathbf{K}}\mathbf{x} - \mathbf{u}\|_2^2 + \phi_{\text{GTV}}(\mathbf{x}) \tag{8}$$

where $\hat{\mathbf{K}}$ is the convolution matrix constructed by $\hat{\mathbf{k}}$ obtained from the blur filter estimation below.

5. ► Update the blur filter estimate

$$\hat{\mathbf{k}} \leftarrow \arg\min_{\mathbf{k}} \tfrac{\lambda}{2}\|\hat{\mathbf{X}}\mathbf{k} - \mathbf{u}\|_2^2 + \iota_{\mathcal{S}}(\mathbf{k}) \tag{9}$$

where $\hat{\mathbf{X}}$ is the convolution matrix constructed by $\hat{\mathbf{x}}$ obtained from the image estimation above.

6. ► Increase the parameter λ

$$\lambda \leftarrow \alpha\lambda. \tag{10}$$

7. **Step III**: Non-blind estimation of HR image $\mathbf{x}^*$ from $\mathbf{u}$ through solving (8) with final $\hat{\mathbf{h}}$ (obtained by Step II).
8. **Output**: the HR image $\mathbf{x}^*$ and the blur estimate $\hat{\mathbf{h}}$.

To avoid getting trapped in a local minimum, above algorithmic framework is implemented in a coarse-to-fine fashion as [26][29][30][31]. The sub-problems (8) and (9) can be solved by many existing methods, and next we show how these two sub-problems can be efficiently solved by the ADMM.

C. The ADMM

Before proceeding, we first introduce the ADMM [21][22], which has been as a popular tool to solve imaging inverse problems (see [27][32] and references therein), and is well suited for addressing the general unconstrained minimization problem composed of J sub-functions:

$$\min_{\mathbf{x}} \sum_j^J g_j(\mathbf{B}^{(j)}\mathbf{x}) \tag{11}$$

where $\mathbf{B}^{(j)}$ are arbitrary matrices and g_j are functions. The ADMM to solve (11) takes the following form (see [32]):

Algorithm *ADMM for solving (11)*

1. Set $k = 0$, $\beta > 0$, $\mathbf{v}_0^{(1)}, \cdots, \mathbf{v}_0^{(J)}$, $\mathbf{d}_0^{(1)}, \cdots, \mathbf{d}_0^{(J)}$.
2. **repeat**
3. $\quad \mathbf{r}_k = \sum_{j=1}^J (\mathbf{B}^{(j)})^T(\mathbf{v}_k^{(j)} + \mathbf{d}_k^{(j)})$
4. $\quad \mathbf{x}_{k+1} = \left[\sum_{j=1}^J (\mathbf{B}^{(j)})^T\mathbf{B}^{(j)}\right]^{-1} \mathbf{r}_k$
5. $\quad$ **for** $j = 1, \cdots, J$
6. $\quad\quad \mathbf{v}_{k+1}^{(j)} = \text{Prox}_{g_j/\tau}\left(\mathbf{B}^{(j)}\mathbf{x}_{k+1} - \mathbf{d}_k^{(j)}\right)$
7. $\quad\quad \mathbf{d}_{k+1}^{(j)} = \mathbf{d}_k^{(j)} - (\mathbf{B}^{(j)}\mathbf{x}_{k+1} - \mathbf{v}_{k+1}^{(j)})$
8. $\quad$ **end for**
9. $\quad k \leftarrow k + 1$
10. **until** some stopping criterion is satisfied.

In line 6 of above algorithm, the proximity operator of g_j/τ: $\text{Prox}_{g_j/\tau}$ is defined as

$$\text{Prox}_{g_j/\tau}(\mathbf{v}) = \arg\min_{\mathbf{x}} \left(g_j(\mathbf{x}) + \frac{\tau}{2}\|\mathbf{x} - \mathbf{v}\|^2\right). \tag{12}$$

Next, we tackle the sub-problems (8) and (9) using the ADMM.

D. x update using the ADMM

The sub-problem (8) can be written in the form (11), with

$$g_1(\cdot) = \tfrac{\lambda}{2}\|\cdot - \mathbf{u}\|_2^2,\; g_2(\cdot) = g_3(\cdot) = \|\cdot\|_p^p, \tag{13}$$

$$\mathbf{B}^{(1)} = \hat{\mathbf{K}},\; \mathbf{B}^{(2)} = \mathbf{D}_h,\; \mathbf{B}^{(3)} = \mathbf{D}_v \tag{14}$$

then solving (8) using the ADMM yields the following algorithm:

Algorithm *ADMM for solving (8)*

1. **Initialize** $k = 0$, $\tau_1 > 0$, $\mathbf{v}_0^{(1)}, \mathbf{v}_0^{(2)}, \mathbf{v}_0^{(3)}$, $\mathbf{d}_0^{(1)}, \mathbf{d}_0^{(2)}, \mathbf{d}_0^{(3)}$.
2. **repeat**
3. $\quad \mathbf{z}_k^{(1)} = \mathbf{v}_k^{(1)} + \mathbf{d}_k^{(1)}$
4. $\quad \mathbf{z}_k^{(2)} = \mathbf{v}_k^{(2)} + \mathbf{d}_k^{(2)}$
5. $\quad \mathbf{z}_k^{(3)} = \mathbf{v}_k^{(3)} + \mathbf{d}_k^{(3)}$
6. $\quad \mathbf{r}_k = \hat{\mathbf{K}}^T\mathbf{z}_k^{(1)} + \mathbf{D}_h^T\mathbf{z}_k^{(2)} + \mathbf{D}_h^T\mathbf{z}_k^{(3)}$
7. $\quad \mathbf{x}_{k+1} = \left[\hat{\mathbf{K}}^T\hat{\mathbf{K}} + \mathbf{D}_h^T\mathbf{D}_h + \mathbf{D}_v^T\mathbf{D}_v\right]^{-1} \mathbf{r}_k$

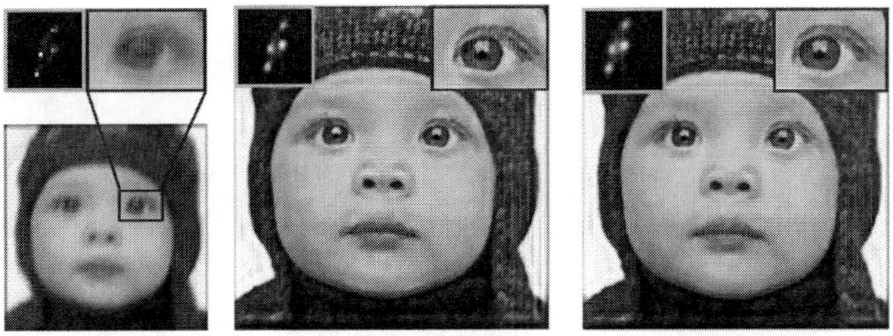

Figure 1. Estimated HR images (size: 512×512), PSFs and PSNRs. (a) are input LR blurry image (size: 256×256, obtained by (1)) and one of the eight PSFs (corresponding to $\mathbf{B}$); (b) and (c) are estimated HR images, PSFs (corresponding to $\mathbf{K}$) and PSNRs by the proposed method with the *bicubic* and *bilinear* interpolation operators, respectively.

Other seven PSFs								
bicubic	Estimated PSFs							
	PSNR (dB)	**20.809**	17.228	**16.856**	21.171	16.512	17.040	**16.364**
bilinear	Estimated PSFs							
	PSNR (dB)	19.933	**19.213**	16.569	**22.184**	**16.776**	**17.454**	16.286

Figure 2. Other seven PSFs and their corresponding estimated PSFs and PSNRs by the proposed method with the *bicubic* and *bilinear* operators, respectively.

8. $\mathbf{v}_{k+1}^{(1)} = \text{Prox}_{g_1/\tau_1}\left(\hat{\mathbf{K}}\mathbf{x}_{k+1} - \mathbf{d}_k^{(1)}\right)$
9. $\mathbf{d}_{k+1}^{(1)} = \mathbf{d}_k^{(1)} - (\hat{\mathbf{K}}\mathbf{x}_{k+1} - \mathbf{v}_{k+1}^{(1)})$
10. $\mathbf{v}_{k+1}^{(2)} = \text{Prox}_{g_2/\tau_1}\left(\mathbf{D}_h\mathbf{x}_{k+1} - \mathbf{d}_k^{(2)}\right)$
11. $\mathbf{d}_{k+1}^{(2)} = \mathbf{d}_k^{(2)} - (\mathbf{D}_h\mathbf{x}_{k+1} - \mathbf{v}_{k+1}^{(2)})$
12. $\mathbf{v}_{k+1}^{(3)} = \text{Prox}_{g_3/\tau_1}\left(\mathbf{D}_v\mathbf{x}_{k+1} - \mathbf{d}_k^{(3)}\right)$
13. $\mathbf{d}_{k+1}^{(3)} = \mathbf{d}_k^{(3)} - (\mathbf{D}_v\mathbf{x}_{k+1} - \mathbf{v}_{k+1}^{(3)})$
14. $k \leftarrow k+1$
15. **until** some stopping criterion is satisfied.

In above algorithm, line 7 is involved by the inversion of the matrix $\hat{\mathbf{K}}^T\hat{\mathbf{K}} + \mathbf{D}_h^T\mathbf{D}_h + \mathbf{D}_v^T\mathbf{D}_v$, which is block-circulant. Thus, it can be digonalzied by 2D *discrete Fourier transform* (DFT) with $\mathcal{O}(n\log n)$ cost, and the inversion of the resulting diagonal matrix can be computed with $\mathcal{O}(n)$ cost. Line 8 is the proximity operator of g_1/τ_1, which can be obtained in a closed-form:

$$\mathbf{v}_{k+1}^{(1)} = \frac{\lambda\mathbf{u} + \tau_1(\hat{\mathbf{K}}\mathbf{x}_{k+1} - \mathbf{d}_k^{(1)})}{\lambda + \tau_1}; \tag{15}$$

line 10 and 12 are the proximity operators of the ℓ_p $(0 \leq p \leq 1)$ norm, and they have closed-form solutions for $p \in \{0, \frac{1}{2}, \frac{2}{3}, 1, \frac{4}{3}, \frac{3}{2}, 2\}$ (see [33]). For other general p, no closed-form solution exists, but it can be pre-computed numerically and used in the form of lookup table as that in [28].

E. k *update using the ADMM*

In the same vein as above, the sub-problem (9) can be written in the form (11), with

$$g_1(\cdot) = \tfrac{\lambda}{2}\left\|\cdot - \mathbf{u}\right\|_2^2, \; g_2(\cdot) = \iota_S(\cdot), \tag{16}$$

$$\mathbf{B}^{(1)} = \hat{\mathbf{X}}, \; \mathbf{B}^{(2)} = \mathbf{I}, \tag{17}$$

yielding the following algorithm:

Algorithm *ADMM for solving (9)*
1. **Initialize** $k = 0$, $\tau_2 > 0$, $\mathbf{v}_0^{(1)}, \mathbf{v}_0^{(2)}, \mathbf{d}_0^{(1)}, \mathbf{d}_0^{(2)}$.
2. **repeat**
3. $\mathbf{z}_k^{(1)} = \mathbf{v}_k^{(1)} + \mathbf{d}_k^{(1)}$
4. $\mathbf{z}_k^{(2)} = \mathbf{v}_k^{(2)} + \mathbf{d}_k^{(2)}$
5. $\mathbf{r}_k = \hat{\mathbf{X}}^T\mathbf{z}_k^{(1)} + \mathbf{z}_k^{(2)}$
6. $\mathbf{k}_{k+1} = \left[\hat{\mathbf{X}}^T\hat{\mathbf{X}} + \mathbf{I}\right]^{-1}\mathbf{r}_k$
7. $\mathbf{v}_{k+1}^{(1)} = \text{Prox}_{g_1/\tau_2}\left(\hat{\mathbf{X}}\mathbf{k}_{k+1} - \mathbf{d}_k^{(1)}\right)$
8. $\mathbf{d}_{k+1}^{(1)} = \mathbf{d}_k^{(1)} - (\hat{\mathbf{X}}\mathbf{k}_{k+1} - \mathbf{v}_{k+1}^{(1)})$
9. $\mathbf{v}_{k+1}^{(2)} = \text{Prox}_{g_2/\tau_2}\left(\mathbf{k}_{k+1} - \mathbf{d}_k^{(2)}\right)$
10. $\mathbf{d}_{k+1}^{(2)} = \mathbf{d}_k^{(2)} - (\mathbf{k}_{k+1} - \mathbf{v}_{k+1}^{(2)})$
11. $k \leftarrow k+1$
12. **until** some stopping criterion is satisfied.

In line 6, the matrix $\hat{\mathbf{X}}^T\hat{\mathbf{X}}+\mathbf{I}$ can also be diagonalized by DFT with $\mathcal{O}(n\log n)$ cost. Line 7 can be evaluated in a closed-form

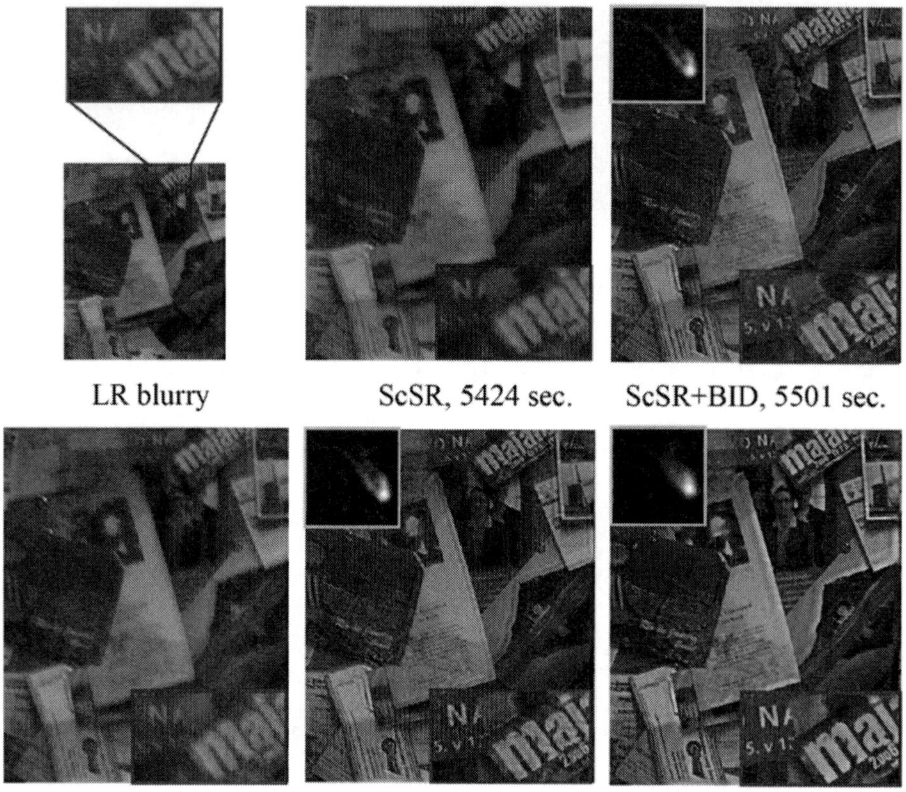

Figure 3. Results on a real LR blurry image, where the LR image size is 900×540 and the HR image size is 1800×1080.

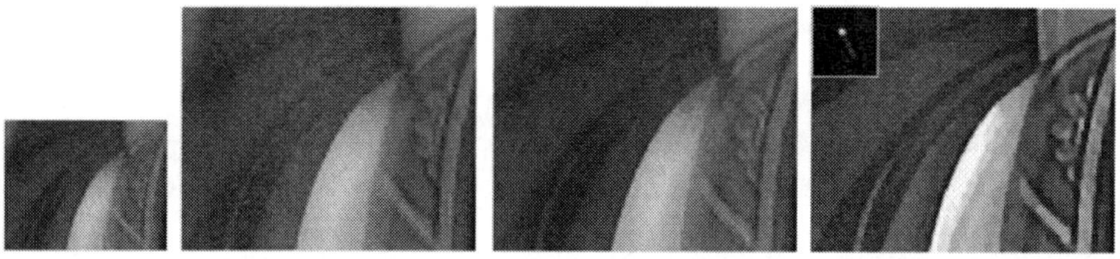

Figure 4. Results on a real LR image, where the LR image size is 324×464 and the HR image size is 648×928.

as (15). Line 9 is the projection onto the probability simplex $\mathcal{S}$ (see (7)), which has been already addressed in [34].

III. Experiments

In this section, we report detailed results of the proposed method. All the experiments were performed using MATLAB on a 64-bit Windows 10 personal computer with an Intel Core i7 2.5 GHz processor and 6.0 GB of RAM. The parameters of proposed method are set as $\lambda = 1, \alpha = 1.5, \tau_1 = \tau_2 = 0.15$ and $p = 0.5$, and the setups of involved state-of-the-art methods remain unchanged as their original ones. The BID flow for a color image is: (1) first, convert the image from RGB color space to YCbCr color space, (2) BID of the luminance channel, and (3) convert the image back to the RGB color space. The stopping criterion is chose as $||\hat{\mathbf{f}}_{k+1} - \hat{\mathbf{f}}_k||/||\hat{\mathbf{f}}_{k+1}|| \leq 0.0001$ where $\hat{\mathbf{f}}_k$ is the image estimate or kernel estimate at the k-th iteration. Other parameters are set by following those in [27]. Other details are shown as follows:

A. *On synthetic blurry images*

In this sub-section, we tested our algorithm on the Baby image (size: 512×512) blurred by eight PSFs of true motion blur provided by [35]. In the algorithm, the operator $\mathbf{U}$ has two options: the *bicubic* and *bilinear* interpolation operators. For saving space, we only show the results on the image blurred by one PSF in Fig. 1, and the results with other seven PSFs are shown in Fig. 2. Notice that PSNR is defined as $20\log_{10}(255/\sqrt{\text{MSE}})$ where MSE is the mean squared-error between the luminance channel of the original Baby image and the restored HR one. Fig. 1 and 2 verify the rationality of reformulating SBISR into BID (see (5)).

B. On real images

We also tested our algorithm (only with the *bilinear* interpolation operator due to space limitation) on real images, comparing with state-of-the-art SISR methods: ScSR [8] and SRCNN [36]. Since we currently cannot get access to any SBISR code, we add the proposed BID algorithm as a post-process of the two SISR methods on a real LR blurry image, and the results are shown in Fig. 3. For the sake of fair comparison, we further run the proposed method and the SISR methods on a LR image (not blurry), and the results are shown in Fig. 4. From Fig. 3 and 4, we can see the competitiveness of the proposed method, both in terms of speed and restoration quality, on LR blurry and non-blurry images.

IV. CONCLUSION

We have proposed a new approach for *single blind image super-resolution* (SBISR) via a *blind image deblurring* (BID) method, bridging the gap between SBISR and BID. Experiments on synthetic and real blurry images (also on a real sharp image) show that the effectiveness and competitiveness of the proposed method. Future work will involve exploiting the influence of using advanced interpolation operators on the proposed method.

REFERENCES

[1] H. Chang, D. Y. Yeung, and Y. Xiong, "Super-resolution through neighbor embedding," in IEEE CVPR, 2004, pp. 275–282.

[2] R. Fattal, "Image upsampling via imposed edge statistics," ACM ToG, 2007, vol. 26, pp. 95.

[3] W. Freeman, T. Jones, and E. Pasztor, "Example-based super-resolution," Computer grahics and Applications, vol. 22, no. 2.

[4] S. Mallat and G. Yu, "Super-resolution with sparse mixing estimators," IEEE TSP, vol. 19, 2010, pp. 2889–2900.

[5] J. Yang, J. Wright, T. Huang, and Y. Ma, "Image super-resolution as sparse representation of raw image patches," in IEEE CVPR, 2008.

[6] R. Zeyde, M. Elad, and M. Protter, "On single image scale-up using sparse-representations," Curves and Surfaces, 2012.

[7] D. Glasner, S. Bagon, and M. Irani, "Super-resolution from a single image," in ICCV, 2009, pp. 349–356.

[8] J. Yang, J. Wright, T. S. Huang, and Y. Ma, "Image super-resolution via sparse representation," IEEE TIP, vol. 19, 2010, pp. 2961–2873.

[9] F. Farsiu, D. Robinson, M. Elad, and P. Milanfar, "Fast and roubst multi-frame super-resolution," IEEE TIP, vol. 13, 2003, pp. 1327–1344.

[10] F. Šroubek, G. Cristóbal, and J. Flusser, "A unified approach to superresolution and multichannel blind deconvolution," IEEE TIP, vol. 19, 2010, pp. 2961–2873.

[11] Y. Romano, M. Protter, and M. Elad, "Sparse representation based image interpolation with nonlocal autoregressive modeling," IEEE TIP, vol. 22, 2013, pp. 1382–1394.

[12] X. Zhang and X. Wu, "Image interpolation by adaptive 2-d autoregressive modeling and soft-decision estimation," IEEE TIP, vol. 17, 2008, pp. 887–896.

[13] I. Bégin and F. Ferrie, "Blind super-resolution using a learning-based approach," in ICPR, 2004.

[14] W. Freeman and C. Liu, "Markow random fields for super-resolution and texture synthesis," in Advances in Markov Random Fields for Vision and Image Processing, 2011.

[15] J. Qiao, J. Liu, and C. Zhao, "A novel svm-based blind super-resolution algorithm," in International Joint Conference on Neural Networks, 2006.

[16] Q. Wang, X. Tang, and H. Shum, "Patch based blind image super-resolution," in ICCV, 2005.

[17] Y. He, K. H Yap, L. Chen, and L. P. Chau, "A soft map framework for blind super-resolution reconstruction," Image and Vision Computing, vol. 27, 2009, pp. 364–373.

[18] N. Joshi, R. Szeliski, and D. J. Kriegman, "Psf estimation using sharp edge prediction," in IEEE CVPR, 2008.

[19] N. Efrat, D. Glasner, A. Apartsin, B. Nadler, and A. Levin, "Accurate blur models vs. image priors in single image super-resolution," in ICCV, 2013.

[20] T. Michaeli and M. Irani, "Nonparametric blind super-resolution," in ICCV, 2013.

[21] D. Gabay and B. Mercier, "A dual algorithm for the solution of nonlinear variational problems via nite element approximations," Computers and Mathematics with Applications, vol. 2, 1976, pp. 17–40.

[22] S. Boyd, N. Parikh, E. Chu, B. Peleato, and J. Eckstein, "Distributed optimization and statistical learning via the alternating direction method of multipliers," Foundations and Trends in Machine Learning, vol. 3, 2011, pp. 1–122.

[23] R. Fergus, B. Singh, A. Hertzmann, S. Roweis and W. Freeman, "Removing camera shake from a single photograph," in ACM Transactons on Graph, 2006, pp. 787–794.

[24] P. Campisi and K. Egiazarian, "Blind image deconvolution: theory and applications," in CRC press., 2007.

[25] L. Xu and J. Jia, "Two-phase kernel estimation for robust motion deblurring," in ECCV, 2010, pp. 157–170.

[26] J. Kotera, F. Sroubek, and P. Milanfar, "Blind deconvolution using alternating maximum a posteriori estimation with heavy-tailed priors," in Computer Analysis of Images and Patterns, Lecture Notes in Computer Science, vol. 8048, 2013, pp. 59–66.

[27] M. S. C. Almeida, and M. A. T. Figueiredo, "Blind image deblurring with unknown boundaries using the alternating direction method of multipliers," ICIP, 2013, pp. 586–590.

[28] D. Krishnan, and R. Fergus, "Fast image deconvolution using hyper-laplacian priors", 2009.

[29] S. Cho and S. Lee, "Fast motion deblurring," ACM ToG, vol. 28, 2009.

[30] C. Wang, L. Sun, Z. Chen, J. Zhang, and S. Yang, "Multi-scale blind motion deblurring using local minimum," Inverse Problems, vol. 26, 2010, pp. 015003.

[31] D. Krishnan, T. Tay, and R. Fergus, "Blind deconvolution using a normalized sparsity measure," in IEEE CVPR, 2011, pp. 233–240.

[32] M. V. Afonso, J. M. Bioucas-Dias, and M. A. T. Figueiredo, "An augmented lagrangian approach to the constrained optimization formulation of imaging inverse problems," IEEE TIP, vol. 20, 2011, pp. 681–695.

[33] P. L. Combettes and V. R. Wajs, "Signal recovery by proximal forward-backward splitting," Multiscale Modeling & Simulation, vol. 4, 2005, pp. 1168–1200.

[34] J. Duchi, S. Shalev-Shwartz, Y. Singer, and T. Chandra, "Efficient projections onto the l1-ball for learning in high dimensions," in Proc. 25th international conference on Machine learning, 2008, pp. 272–279.

[35] A. Levin, Y. Weiss, F. Durand, and W. T. Freeman, "Understanding and evaluating blind deconvolution algorithms," in IEEE CVPR, 2009, pp. 1964–1971.

[36] C. Dong, C. C. Loy, K. He, and X. Tang, "Learning a deep convolution network for image super-resolution," in ECCV, 2014.

Tongue Recognition From Images

Ryszard S. Choraś

Institute of Telecommunications and Computer Science
UTP University of Sciences and Technology
85-796 Bydgoszcz, Poland
Email: choras@utp.edu.pl

Abstract—**This paper proposes a method of personal identification based on tongue image. Tongue images have many advantage for personal identification and verification. In this paper a texture tongue features are extracted based on Gabor filters, and *WLD* (Weber Law Descriptors) transform. These features can be used in forensic applications and with other robust biometrics features can be combined in multi modal biometric system.**

Keywords*—*Tongue image, Gabor filters, Weber Law Descriptors.

I. Introduction

Tongue recognition is attracting a great deal of attention because of its usefulness in many applications. Traditional, tongue recognition are often classified into two groups:

- Tongue recognition and analysis for the patient disease diagnosis. Tongue recognition for diagnosis has played an important role in traditional Chinese medicine (*TCM*) and in this area most investigation has been focused on extraction of chromatic features [11] [16], shape and textural features [7] [8] [12].
- Tongue recognition for biometric personal identification.

Our work concerns the biometric applications of the tongue recognition and efficient feature extraction.
Biometrics human identifications uses automated methods of recognizing a person based on a physiological or behavioral characteristics [6]. A biometric system is a pattern recognition system that recognizes a person on the basis of a feature vector derived from a specific physiological or behavioral characteristics that the person possesses. Physiological Biometrics - also known as static biometrics - is based on the data derived from the measurement of a part of a person's anatomy [9].

Tongue image analysis have received much attention in image analysis and computer vision. Tongue texture has many advantages for human identification and verification [10] [18]. The identification of people can be based on the texture features. As a biometric identifier, tongue image has the following properties:

- Tongue images are unique to every person. Texture features of the tongue are distinctive to each person,
- Texture features of an individual tongue are stable and unchangeable during the life of a person,
- The human tongue is well protected in mouth and is difficult to forge.

Tongue recognition system is presented in Figure 1 and it involves five major modules: tongue image acquisition, preprocessing, tongue feature extraction, visual features and classification.

In this paper, a tongue image feature extraction method is proposed, which utilizes Gabor filters and local features such as *WLD*, because these features are robust against some types of geometric modifications. Weber local descriptors (*WLD*) is a simple but powerful local descriptor, which simulates the human visual perception.

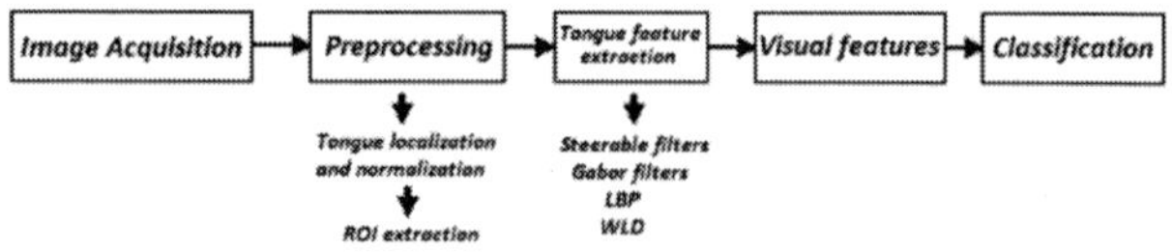

Fig. 1. Tongue recognition system

Images which are considered in this paper are displayed in Figure 2.

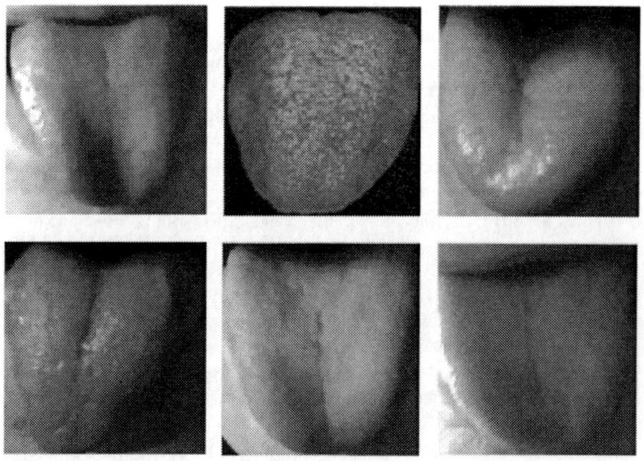

Fig. 2. Tongue images

The remainder of this paper is organized as follows. Section 2 briefly describes the preprocessing operations. In Section 3, we describe Gabor filters, propose a local descriptor called *WLD* and briefly describes the definition of Weber magnitude and orientation. Conclusions and references are given thereafter.

II. PREPROCESSING

Before performing feature extraction, the original tongue images are subjected to some image processing operations, such as:

1) Image stretching. The contrast level is stretched according to

$$f_{out}(x,y) = 255 \times \left(\frac{f_{in}(x,y) - f_{in_{min}}(x,y)}{f_{in_{max}}(x,y) - f_{in_{min}}(x,y)} \right)^{\gamma} \quad (1)$$

$f_{out}(x,y)$ is the color level for the output pixel (x,y) after the contrast stretching process. $f_{in}(x,y)$ is the color level input for data the pixel (x,y). $f_{in_{max}}(x,y)$ - is the maximum value for color level in the input image. $f_{in_{min}}(x,y)$ - is the minimum value for color level in the input image, γ - constant that defines the shape of the stretching curve.

2) Extraction of region of interest *(ROI)* from original tongue images. The tongue images are normalized with respect to position, orientation, scale, reflection, as follows.
The new invariant coordinates (x,y) of image pixels and the old coordinates (x',y') are related by

$$[x, y, 1] = [x', y'1] \times \begin{bmatrix} 1 & 0 & 0 \\ 0 & 1 & 0 \\ -i_0 & -j_0 & 1 \end{bmatrix} \times$$

$$\times \begin{bmatrix} \frac{1}{\delta_x} & 0 & 0 \\ 0 & \frac{1}{\delta_y} & 0 \\ 0 & 0 & 1 \end{bmatrix} \times \begin{bmatrix} \cos\beta & \sin\beta & 0 \\ -\sin\beta & \cos\beta & 0 \\ 0 & 0 & 1 \end{bmatrix} \quad (2)$$

where x_0, y_0 is the centroid of image; δ_x and δ_y represent standard deviation relative to variable x, y; and β is an angle between the major axis of an object and the vertical line

$$\tan 2\beta = \frac{2\sum_x \sum_y (x - x_0)(y - y_0)}{\sum_x (x - x_0^2) - \sum_y (y - y_0^2)} \quad (3)$$

Next, the *ROI*'s tongue blocks are automatically selected on the centroid of tongue normalized images. The size of whole *ROI* is $w_x \times w_y$ where $w_x = (x_0 + \frac{K}{2}) - (x_0 - \frac{K}{2})$, $w_y = (y_0 + \frac{K}{2}) - (y_0 - \frac{K}{2})$ where $K = 128$ pixels (Figure 3). Next, the *ROI* image is divided into the four sub-blocks. The size of sub-block is $\frac{K}{2} \times \frac{K}{2}$ pixels (Figure 4).

III. FEATURE EXTRACTION

A. Gabor filters for feature extraction

Gabor filters are a powerful tool to extract texture features and in the spatial domain is a complex exponential modulated by a Gaussian function. In the most general the Gabor filters are defined as follows [3] [14] [15].

The two-dimensional Gabor filter is defined as

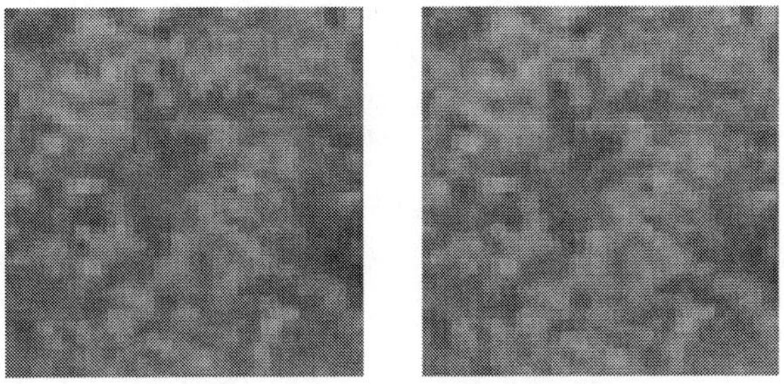

Fig. 3. Tongue *ROI*

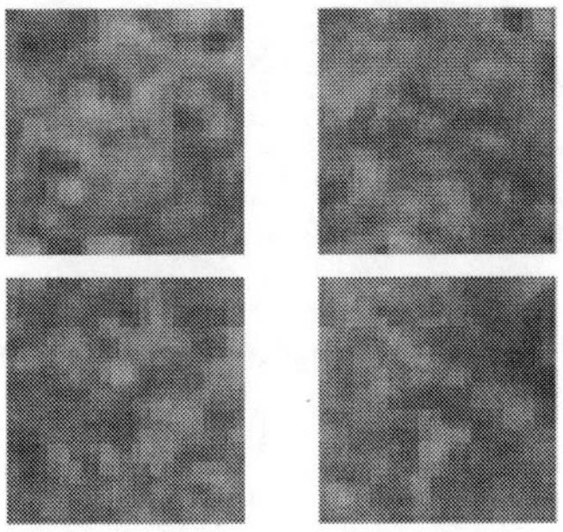

Fig. 4. Four *ROI*'s sub-blocks

$$Gab(x, y, W, \theta, \sigma_x, \sigma_y) =$$

$$= \frac{1}{2\pi\sigma_x\sigma_y} e^{\left[-\frac{1}{2}\left(\left(\frac{x}{\sigma_x}\right)^2 + \left(\frac{y}{\sigma_y}\right)^2 \right) + jW(x\cos\theta + y\sin\theta) \right]} \quad (4)$$

where $j = \sqrt{-1}$ and σ_x and σ_y are the scaling parameters of the filter, W is the radial frequency of the sinusoid and $\theta \in [0, \pi]$ specifies the orientation of the Gabor filters.

Figure 5 presents the real and imaginary parts of Gabor filters.

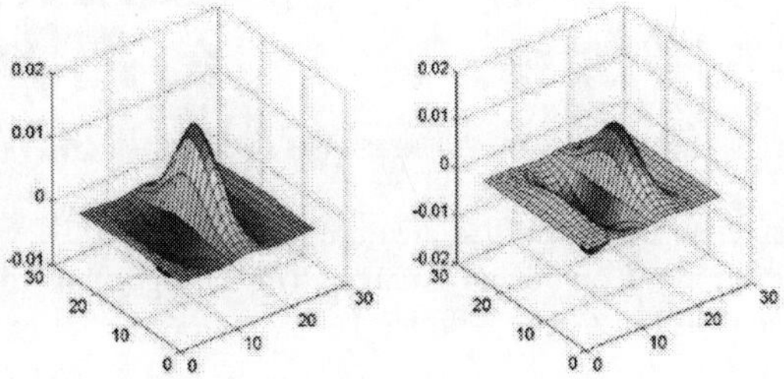

a) b)

Fig. 5. The real and imaginary parts of Gabor filters

In our work we use a bank of filters built from the real part of Gabor expression called as even symmetric Gabor filter. Gabor filtered output of the image is obtained by the convolution of the image with Gabor even function for each of the orientation/spatial frequency (scale) orientation (Figure 6).

Given an image $F(x,y)$, we filter this image with $Gab(x,y,W,\theta,\sigma_x,\sigma_y)$

$$FGab(x,y,W,\theta,\sigma_x,\sigma_y) = \\ = \sum_k \sum_l F(x-k, y-l) * Gab(x,y,W,\theta,\sigma_x,\sigma_y) \quad (5)$$

The magnitudes of the Gabor filters responses are represented by three moments

$$\mu(W,\theta,\sigma_x,\sigma_y) = \frac{1}{XY} \sum_{x=1}^{X} \sum_{y=1}^{Y} FGab(x,y,W,\theta,\sigma_x,\sigma_y) \quad (6)$$

$$std(W,\theta,\sigma_x,\sigma_y) = \\ = \sqrt{\sum_{x=1}^{X} \sum_{y=1}^{Y} ||FGab(x,y,W,\theta,\sigma_x,\sigma_y)| - \mu(W,\theta,\sigma_x,\sigma_y)|^2} \quad (7)$$

$$Energy = \sum_{x=1}^{X} \sum_{y=1}^{Y} [FGab(x,y,W,\theta,\sigma_x,\sigma_y)]^2 \quad (8)$$

By selecting different center frequencies and orientations, we can obtain a family of Gabor kernels, which can then be used to extract features from an image. The feature vector is constructed using *mean* - $\mu(W,\theta,\sigma_x,\sigma_y)$, *standard deviation* - $std(W,\theta,\sigma_x,\sigma_y)$ and *energy* as feature components (Table I).

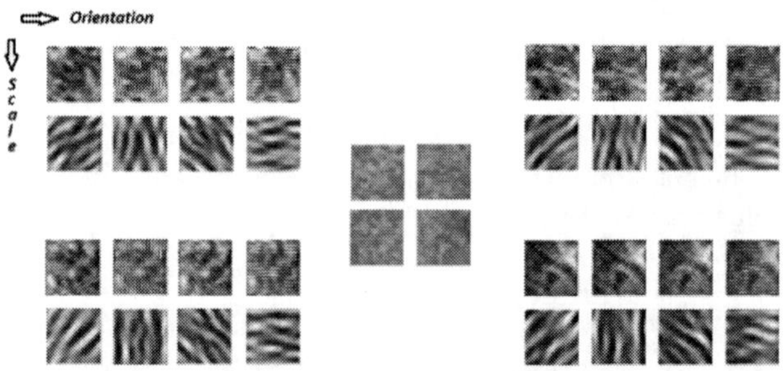

Fig. 6. Gabor images of tongue *ROI*'s

To reduce dimension of feature vector [13], [17], we use the Principle Component Analysis (*PCA*) algorithm to keep the most useful Gabor features.

Let $X = [x_1, x_2, \ldots, x_n]$ denote an n-dimensional feature vector. The mean of the vector X and the total scatter covariance matrix of the vector X are defined as: $\overline{\mu} = \frac{1}{n}\sum_{i=1}^{n} x_i$ and $S_X = \sum_{i=1}^{n}(x_i - \overline{\mu}) \cdot (x_i - \overline{\mu})^t$.

The *PCA* projection matrix S can be obtained by eigenanalysis of the covariance matrix S_X. We compute the eigenvalues of $S_X : \lambda_1 > \lambda_2 > \cdots > \lambda_n$ and the eigenvectors of $S_X : s_1, s_2, \ldots, s_n$. Thus $S_X s_i = \lambda_i s_i, \ \ i = 1, 2, \ldots, m$. s_i is the ith largest eigenvector of S_X, $m \ll n$ and $S = [s_1, s_2, \ldots, s_m]$.

TABLE I. FEATURES OF TONGUE *ROI*'S.

Scale	Orientation	Energy	Mean	Std
ROI 1				
2	45°	1968755.0	480.65308	35.064735
2	90°	1999251.1	488.09842	40.68314
2	135°	1968758.9	480.65402	34.23929
2	180°	1999252.2	488.0987	42.19372
8	45°	3.181323E7	7766.903	669.66876
8	90°	3.1827126E7	7770.2944	657.5264
8	135°	3.181321E7	7766.897	762.5107
8	180°	3.1827142E7	7770.2983	728.3237
ROI 2				
2	45°	1968755.0	480.65308	35.064735
2	90°	1999251.1	488.09842	40.68314
2	135°	1968758.9	480.65402	34.23929
2	180°	1999252.2	488.0987	42.19372
8	45°	3.181323E7	7766.903	669.66876
8	90°	3.1827126E7	7770.2944	657.5264
8	135°	3.181321E7	7766.897	762.5107
8	180°	3.1827142E7	7770.2983	728.3237
ROI 3				
2	45°	1867638.8	455.9665	36.981506
2	90°	1896568.8	463.02948	44.25503
2	135°	1867638.6	455.96646	36.304142
2	180°	1896567.2	463.0291	41.741203
8	45°	3.0179278E7	7367.988	707.88116
8	90°	3.0192456E7	7371.205	717.7458
8	135°	3.0179264E7	7367.984	774.104
8	180°	3.0192524E7	7371.221	614.612
ROI 4				
2	45°	1906920.6	465.5568	27.945246
2	90°	1936458.5	472.7682	35.911766
2	135°	1906919.8	465.55658	28.149256
2	180°	1936459.8	472.7685	35.161488
8	45°	3.0813984E7	7522.9453	786.99506
8	90°	3.08275E7	7526.245	728.3674
8	135°	3.0814002E7	7522.9497	562.7714
8	180°	3.082751E7	7526.2476	521.4142

Any vector x can be written as a linear combination of the eigenvectors (S is symmetric, $s_1, s_2, \ldots, s_n$form a basis), i.e. $x = \sum_{i=1}^{n} b_i u_i$. For dimensionality reduction we choose only m largest eigen values, i.e. $x = \sum_{i=1}^{m} b_i u_i$. m is choose as follows: $\frac{\sum_{i=1}^{m}\lambda_i}{\sum_{i=1}^{n}\lambda_i} > t$ where t is threshold.

By removing the principal components that contribute little to the variance, we project the entire feature vector to a lower dimensional space, but retain most of the information.

B. Weber Law Descriptors

In 1834 Ernst Weber stated that "the ratio between the smallest perceptual change in a stimulus $\triangle f_{min}$ and the background level of the stimulus f is constant e.g. $\frac{\triangle f_{min}}{f} = k$" [6]. Inspired by Weber's Law, a robust and powerful Weber Local Descriptor (WLD) is a recently developed for local feature extraction. For each pixel of the input image, we compute two joint descriptors: a differential excitation DE operator and a gradient orientation GO descriptor. The DE is a function of the ratio between two terms: one is the relative intensity differences of a current pixel against its neighbors (e.g., 3×3 square region) and the other is the intensity of the current pixel. The orientation component is the GO of the current pixel. Figure 7 show how the DE and GO are calculated [1].

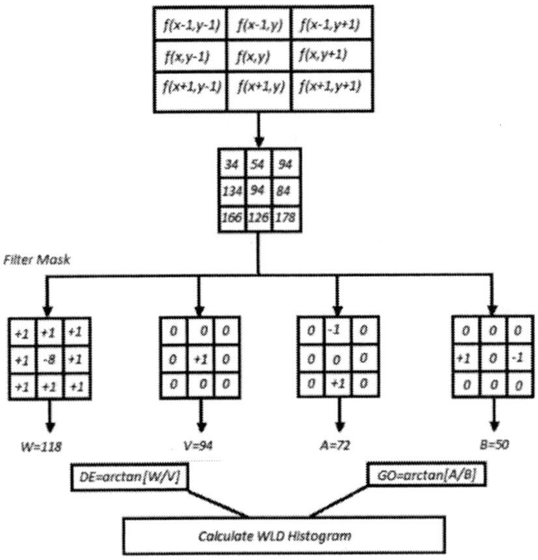

Fig. 7. Illustration of the WLD algorithm

If $f(x,y)$ is the center pixel of a 3×3 window, and $f(x+i, y+j)$; $i = -1, 0, 1$ $j = -1, 0, 1$ are the neighbors of the center pixel, DE is calculated as

$$DE = \arctan\left[\frac{\sum_{i=-1}^{1}\sum_{j=-1}^{1} f(x+i, y+j) - 8f(x,y)}{f(x,y)}\right] = \arctan\left[\frac{W}{V}\right] \quad (9)$$

where: $f(x+i, y+j)$ $i = -1, 0, 1$; $j = -1, 0, 1$ is the gray level intensity of the corresponding pixel. The positive value of DE indicates that the current pixel is darker than the neighboring pixel,while the negative value represents the opposite.

The main purpose of the DE component is to extract the local salient patterns from the image.

The GO of the center pixel $f(x,y)$ is calculated as

$$GO = \arctan\left[\frac{f(i,j-1) - f(i,j+1)}{f(i+1,j) - f(i-1,j)}\right] = \arctan\left[\frac{A}{B}\right] \quad (10)$$

where the numerator is the intensity difference between the left and the right of $f(x,y)$, while the denominator is the intensity difference between the below and the above of $f(x,y)$. Next, the GO are quantized into dominant orientations as follows:

$$GO' = \arctan 2\left[\frac{A}{B} + \pi\right] \quad (11)$$

$$\arctan 2\left[\frac{A}{B}\right] = \begin{cases} GO & A > 0 \ and \ B > 0 \\ \pi - GO & A > 0 \ and \ B < 0 \\ GO - \pi & A < 0 \ and \ B < 0 \\ -GO & A < 0 \ and \ B > 0 \end{cases} \quad (12)$$

The GO is then quantized into T dominant orientations. For each dominant orientation, histogram, H, is calculated using the DE (Figure 8) [1].

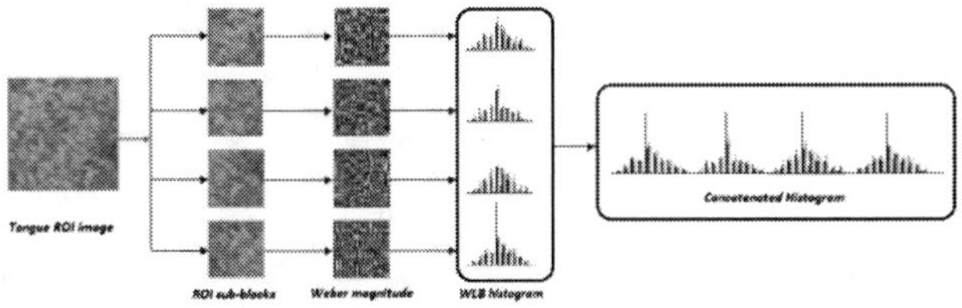

Fig. 8. Tongue feature extraction

Because not all the features are equally important, the feature selection technique is used.

To compute the distance of two histograms chi-square χ^2 distance is used

$$\chi^2(H^1, H^2) = \sum_i \frac{(h_i^1 - h_i^2)^2}{h_i^1 + h_i^2} \quad (13)$$

where H^1 and H^2 are two histograms and h_i^1 , h_i^2 are the ith bin of the histograms.

IV. Conclusion

In the paper, are presented some approaches for tongue recognition from images. To evaluate the performance of tongue recognition methods we use own tongue database that consists 30 images. We proposed a method which combines the recognition results of Gabor filters and *WLD* features to tongue recognition. The *WLD* texture features are robust against rotation and noise. The proposed system will be evaluated on other tongue databases in the future study.

Acknowledgment

The research was supported by the UTP University of Sciences and Technology by the Grant BS01/2014.

References

[1] J. Chen, S. Shan, C. He, G. Zhao, M. Pietikinen, X. Chen, W. Gao, "WLD: A robust local image descriptor", IEEE Transactions on Pattern Analysis and Machine Intelligence, 32(9), pp. 1705 - 1720, 2010.

[2] R. S. Choras, "Iris-based person identification using Gabor wavelets and moments", Proc. 2009 Int. Conf. on Biometrics and Kansei Engineering ICBAKE, CPS IEEE Computer Society, pp. 55-59, 2009.

[3] R. S. Choras, "Lip-prints feature extraction and recognition", Image Processing & Communications Challenges 3, AISC 102, pp.33-41 , Springer-Verlag Berlin Heidelberg, 2011.

[4] R. S. Choras, "Vascular Biometry", Image Processing & Communications Challenges 6, AISC 313, pp. 21 -28, Springer-Verlag Berlin Heidelberg 2015.

[5] R. S. Choras, "Thermal face recognition", Image Processing & Communications Challenges 7, AISC 389, pp. 37-46, Springer-Verlag Berlin Heidelberg 2016.

[6] A. K. Jain, Fundamentals of a Digital Signal Processing, Prentice-Hall, Englewood Clifts, NJ., 1989.

[7] W. Huang, Z. Yan, J. Xu and L. Zhang, "Analysis of the tongue fur and tongue features by naive bayesian classifier", Proceedings of the Int. Conf. Computer Application and System Modeling, Taiyuan, Oct. 2010, vol. 4, pp. 304-308.

[8] B. Huang, D. Zhang, Y. Li, H. Zhang and N. Li, "Tongue coating image retrieval", Proceedings of the 3rd Int. Conf. Advanced Computer Control, Harbin, Jan. 2011, pp. 292-296.

[9] A. K. Jain, R. Bolle and S. Pankanti, Biometrics: Personal Identification in Networked Society, Kulwer Academic, 1999.

[10] S. Lahmiri, "Recognition of tongueprint textures for personal aAuthentication: A wavelet approach", Journal of Advances in Information Technology, vol.3 ,no.3, pp. 168 - 175, 2012.

[11] C. Li and P. Yuen, "Tongue image matching using color content", Pattern Recogn. 35(2), pp. 407-419, 2002.

[12] W. Li, S. Hu, J. Yao and H. Song, "The separation framework of tongue coating and proper in traditional Chinese medicine", Proceedings of the 7th Int. Conf. Information, Communications and Signal Processing, Macau, Dec. 2009, pp. 1-4.

[13] C. J. Liu and H. Wechsler, "Gabor feature based classification using the enhanced Fisher linear discriminant model for face recognition", IEEE Transactions on Image Processing, vol. 11, no. 4, pp. 467- 476, 2002.

[14] D. H. Liu, K. M. Lam, and L. S. Shen, "Optimal sampling of Gabor features for face recognition", Pattern Recognition Letters, vol. 25, no. 2, pp. 267-276, 2004.

[15] L. Shen and L. Bai, "Face recognition based on Gabor features using kernel methods", Proc. 6th IEEE Conf. on Face and Gesture Recognition Korea, pp. 170-175, 2004.

[16] Y. Wang, J. Yang and Y. Zhou, "Region partition and feature matching based color recognition of tongue image", Pattern Recogn. Lett., 28(1), pp. 11-19, 2007.

[17] B.C. Zhang, S.G. Shan, X.L. Chen and W. Gao, "Histogram of Gabor phase patterns(HGPP): a novel object representation approach for face recogniton", IEEE Trans. Image Processing, 16, pp. 57-68, 2007.

[18] D. Zhang, Z. Liu, J. Yan and P. Shi, "Tongue-print: A novel biometrics pattern", ICB 2007, Springer-Verlag LNCS 4642, pp. 1174 - 1183, 2007.

Impact of Redundancy and Gaussian Filtering on Contourlet-Based Texture Retrieval

Nadia Baaziz and Momar Diop
Département d'Informatique et d'Ingénierie
Université du Québec en Outaouais
101 rue Saint Jean Bosco, Gatineau (Québec), J8X 3X7 Canada
e-mail: nadia.baaziz@uqo.ca; diom31@uqo.ca

Abstract— **Multiscale image representations, such as contourlets and wavelets are crucial to significant feature extraction for texture retrieval. In this paper, the aim is to highlight the positive impact of added redundancy and Gaussian filtering in multiscale image decompositions for texture retrieval. Using energy-based retrieval framework on Vistex database, conducted experiments on five multiscale transforms (contourlets, wavelets and their redundant counterparts), show the competitive enhancement provided by the redundant contourlet decomposition in terms of discriminant features and improvement of retrieval rates.**

Keywords*— texture retrieval; contourlet; feature extraction.*

I. INTRODUCTION

Retrieving image data from large scale databases lead to great challenging issues in the research field of content-based image retrieval (CBIR). A special attention is given to texture retrieval because of the omnipresence of this visual feature in most real-world images [1]. Textures are prominent in natural images (as in grasslands, brick walls, fabrics, biological tissues, etc.) and many important image properties are revealed through texture analysis such as granularity, smoothness, coarseness, periodicity, geometric structure, orientation and so on [2]. Therefore, texture retrieval is relevant to CBIR since texture characteristics are powerful in discriminating between images. Successful texture retrieval relies strongly on relevant texture feature extraction and effective similarity measurement steps yielding to high image retrieval accuracy while preserving low level of computational complexity.

There are renowned methodologies for texture feature extraction operating in the spatial domain (e.g., gray level co-occurrence matrices), in the frequency domain (e.g., Fourier spectrum measurements), or in the spatial-frequency domain (e.g., energy of wavelet coefficients) [1].

Spatial-frequency transforms, also known as multiscale representations, decompose the image spectrum into a set of localized frequency-partitions exhibiting image details at multiple scales and directions. Linear filter banks and down-sampling operators are the main tools to perform such decompositions yielding various image representations with specific properties such as multiple scales, frequency selectivity, directionality, redundancy or compactness, perfect reconstruction and shift invariance. The redundancy property is directly related to the amount of oversampling at the decomposition stage. Non-subsampled decompositions are known to be completely redundant and shift invariant. Examples of multiscale transforms include discrete wavelets, Laplacian pyramids and contourlets.

Recent studies have reported the achievement of remarkable outcomes due to the development of a variety of new texture feature extraction techniques operating on these multiscale representations [3][4][5]. This probably was motivated by two main facts: a) the human visual system adequacy to the spatial-frequency representation of image signals, and b) the inherent nature of texture patterns in terms of presence of edges, relation between primitive texture elements and variation in scales and orientations [1][2].

The major contribution of this paper is to study and reveal the benefits of incorporating redundancy and Gaussian filtering in multiscale image transforms for texture feature extraction and retrieval. The remainder of this paper is organized as follows. Section II recalls the main properties of discrete wavelet, discrete contourlet and their redundant variants that are subject to exploration in this work. A special focus is made on redundancy properties. Section III details the incorporated feature extraction methods and the texture retrieval framework. Section IV discusses experimental results and main achievements while Section V concludes the paper.

II. MULTISCALE TEXTURE REPRESENTATION

A. *Discrete wavelets and stationary wavelet transforms*

The discrete wavelet transform (DWT) is efficiently implemented by means of iterative linear filtering and critical down-sampling of the original image yielding three high-frequency sub-bands at each scale level in addition to one low-frequency sub-band usually known as image approximation. The DWT provides a highly compact image representation, that is, the transform is orthogonal, and incorporated down-sampling rates result into a total number of wavelet coefficients equal to the image size. Since its development, the DWT gave rise to many renowned methods and techniques in various fields of image processing and particularly in image compression. However, its use for texture analysis has revealed some limitations in capturing relevant information. In fact, major drawbacks were reported in many studies; lack of shift invariance, poor frequency selectivity and poor directionality (only horizontal, vertical and diagonal orientations).

The stationary wavelet transform (SWT) has been introduced as an improved extension of the DWT. This non-subsampled variant is implemented through the so-called "algorithme à trous" in French (word trous translates into holes in English). The SWT achieves shift invariance property at the cost of substantial redundancy of wavelet coefficients. Indeed, the L-level SWT representation of a $K \times M$ image results into one approximation sub-band and $3L$ detail sub-bands. Thus, total number of wavelet coefficients is equal to $(3L+1)KM$.

B. Standard contourlet transform(SCT)

The discrete contourlet transform as introduced in [6] is designated here as the standard contourlet transform (SCT). Multi-Directionality, non-separable 2-D filtering and small amount of redundancy are among the new ingredients in this geometric transform. The decomposition is performed with high computational efficiency by combining two distinct stages. First, a multiscale decomposition uses a Laplacian pyramid (LP) scheme to transform the image into one coarse version plus a set of Laplacian sub-images. Second, a directional stage (DFB) applies iteratively 2-D filtering (DFB) and critical subsampling to further partition each LP sub-band into different and flexible numbers of frequency wedge-shaped sub-bands, thus capturing geometric structures and directional information in natural images.

When compared to the DWT, the SCT with its extra feature of directionality is almost critically sampled with a small redundancy factor up to 4/3 due to the Laplacian pyramid. SCT leads to efficient representation of smooth object boundaries with a small number of local coefficients in the right directional sub-bands.

C. Nonsubsampled contourlet transform (NSCT)

NSCT is a non-subsampled variant of the SCT [7]. All down-sampling operations are di carded from decomposition stages thus eliminating aliasing problems and allowing for full shift-invariance. However, major drawback lies in the rapid increase of computational cost as large number of directional sub-bands are generated. For example, the NSCT of a $K \times M$ image with 3 scale levels and 4 directions per level results into one approximation sub-band and 3×4 directional sub-bands. Thus, total number of wavelet coefficients is equal to $13KM$ since each sub-band size is the same as original image size.

D. Redundant contourlet transform (RCT)

The redundant contourlet transform (RCT) has been introduced in [8][9]. The RCT variant aims at reducing aliasing problems in SCT by discarding sub-sampling operations and allowing for more redundancy in the multiscale decomposition scheme (see Fig. 1).

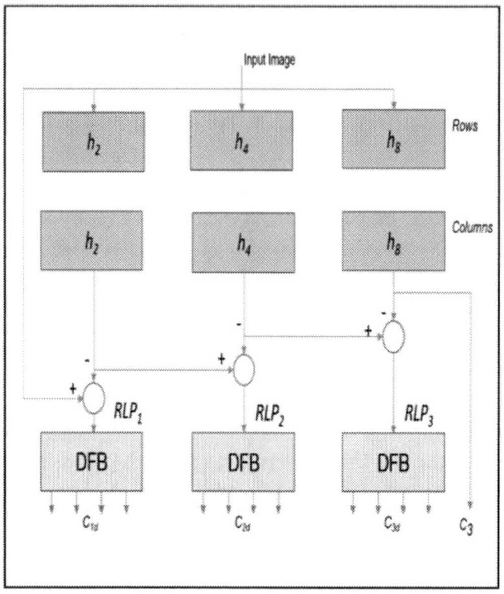

Figure 1. RCT block diagram (3 scale levels) and its frequency partition. Down-sampling is discarded from the Laplacian stage.

As for the standard contourlet transform, the RCT decomposition scheme is divided into two parts: a multiscale decomposition and a directional filter bank (DFB) using two-dimensional filtering and critical down-sampling. While DFB stage is kept unchanged, the multiscale stage is replaced by a redundant Laplacian pyramid (RLP) construct using a set of linear phase low-pass filters with pseudo-Gaussian properties. Filter impulse responses $h_b(n)$ are given in (1) where increasing values of the factor b decreases the filter passband:

$$h_b(n) = e^{-2\left(\frac{n}{b}\right)^2} - e^{-2}\left\{ e^{-2\left(\frac{n-b}{b}\right)^2} + e^{-2\left(\frac{n+b}{b}\right)^2} \right\}. \qquad (1)$$

L filters (with $b=2^l$, $l=1 \dots L$) may be used to build a pyramid having $L+1$ equal-size sub-images: L detail sub-image and one coarse image approximation C_L. Then, a DFB with $D=4$ orientations and $1{:}4$ critical down-sampling is applied on each of the RLP sub-bands to obtain $4L$ equal-size directional sub-bands $\{C_{ld};\ l = 1 \dots L;\ d = 1 \dots D\}$. Thus, the redundancy factor for the RCT is $L+1$ since each RLP sub-band size is the same as original image size.

III. TEXTURE FEATURE EXTRACTION AND RETRIEVAL

Multiscale energy-based approach for texture feature extraction consists in calculating energy (L^1 norm, L^2 norm or some combination of both) and characterizing its distribution through multiscale sub-band images. The energy-based approach assumes that different texture patterns have different energy distribution in the space-frequency domain. This approach is very appealing due to its low computational complexity involving mainly the calculation of first and second order moments of sub-bands coefficients [3]. Given a multiscale decomposition yielding L scale levels and D directional sub-bands C_{ld} at each level, two feature vectors E_1 and E_2 are formed as follow:

$$E(l,d)=\frac{1}{KM}\sum_{i=1}^{K}\sum_{j=1}^{M}\left|C_{ld}(i,j)\right|, \tag{2}$$

$$F(l,d)=\sqrt{\frac{1}{KM}\sum_{i=1}^{K}\sum_{j=1}^{M}\left[C_{ld}(i,j)\right]^2}, \tag{3}$$

$$E_1(l,d)=\left(E(l,d),\ \sqrt{E(l,d)^2+F(l,d)^2}\right), \tag{4}$$

$$E_2(l,d)=\left(E(l,d),F(l,d)\right), \tag{5}$$

$$E_1=\{E_1(l,d);\quad l=1\ldots L; d=1\ldots D\}, \tag{6}$$

$$E_2=\{E_2(l,d);\quad l=1\ldots L; d=1\ldots D\}. \tag{7}$$

With $K{\times}M$ being the size of a given sub-band C_{ld}. Similarity measurement is computed as the Euclidean distance between two compared feature vectors.

Given a database with P images, a visual index is constructed by computing, for each image, its feature vector E_1 (or E_2) as described in (2)-(7). Retrieving similar images to the user query Q is done through the calculation of M Euclidean distances between the query feature vector and the visual index features. The N smallest distances in a ranked order are then selected as *Top-N* matches and corresponding images are retrieved.

IV. Experimental Results

To evaluate the impact of added redundancy and pseudo-Gaussian filtering on the performance of texture retrieval, we conducted experiments using VisTex database [10]. We selected 40 grayscale images from various texture categories (as shown in Fig. 2). Each image of size 512×512 is subdivided into 16 overlapping sub-images of size 256×256, and thus, a database with 640 sub-images is constructed. To avoid any trivial discrimination based on local mean and variance, we normalized grayscale values to zero mean and unit variance. Texture retrieval performance is measured in terms of the retrieval rate (%), which is calculated as the percentage of relevant images found among the *Top-N* retrieved images (with $N=15$).

All retrieval results presented in this paper are obtained by averaging the retrieval rates corresponding to 640 queries. We compared five distinct multiscale transforms combined to two distinct texture retrieval frameworks using energy E_1 and energy E_2 features, respectively. The implemented multiscale decompositions are as follow:

1. DWT: Discrete Wavelet Transform using 4-tap *Daubechies* filters;
2. SWT: Stationary Wavelet Transform using 4-tap *Daubechies* filters;
3. SCT: Standard Contourlet Transform, with *pkva* filters, yielding 4 directional sub-bands at each scale level;
4. NSCT: Non Subsampled Contourlet Transform, with *pkva* filters, yielding 4 directional sub-bands at each scale level;
5. RCT: Redundant Contourlet Transform, with pseudo-Gaussian and *pkva* filters, yielding 4 directional sub-bands at each scale level.

Average retrieval rates (%) obtained by each of the compared methods are given in Table I. In most cases, feature extraction using energy E_2 gives slightly better results than energy E_1. Retrieval is performed with different combinations of scale levels. Each additional scale level increases the performance of the retrieval rate. Top results correspond to 3 scale levels as shown in Table I. The worst retrieval rates are obtained from wavelet-based retrieval (DWT and SWT). This is probably due to the poor directional selectivity of these transforms. We can clearly observe that retrieval rates improve as transform redundancy increases, i.e., SWT leads to better rates than DWT, and NSCT rates are better than SCT ones. However, despite the fact that RCT has a partial redundancy; it yields the best texture retrieval performance (about 3 points higher) thanks to pseudo-Gaussian filters in the Laplacian pyramid stage (see Table II).

The benefit from pseudo-Gaussian filtering is also illustrated in Table III. Indeed, texture retrieval is performed on Laplacian sub-bands, namely, NSCTLap and RCTLap that correspond to the multiscale pyramid stage of NSCT and RCT respectively. Two observations may be drawn from this experiment: 1) retrieval rates are substantially lower than in Table I due to the lack of directional selectivity in the Laplacian decomposition, and 2) performance of RCTLap is better than NSCTLap thanks to pseudo-Gaussian filters, which allow for good texture discrimination.

We believe that, despite the simplicity of the energy-based model for feature extraction, all these successful results in texture retrieval rates have manifested the potential of added redundancy and Gaussian filtering, through RCT, in extracting discriminant texture features.

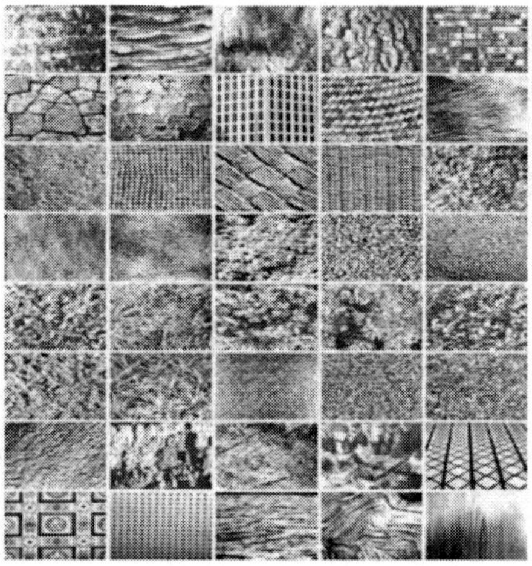

Figure 2. Texture images from the VisTex collection that are used in the experiments; from left to right and top to bottom: Bark0, Bark6, Bark8, Bark9, Brick1, Brick4, Brick5, Buildings9, Fabric0, Fabric4, Fabric7, Fabric9, Fabric11, Fabric14, Fabric15, Fabric17, Fabric18, Flowers5,Food0, Food5, Food8, Grass1, Leaves8, Leaves10, Leaves11, Leaves12, Leaves16, Metal0, Metal2, Misc2, Sand0, Stone1, Stone4, Terrain10, Tile1, Tile4, Tile7, Water5, Wood1, and Wood2.

V. CONCLUSION

The quality of texture retrieval is subject to effective image representation and relevant feature extraction that discriminate among different textures. In this paper, we successfully demonstrated the positive impact of image transform redundancy and Gaussian filtering on the efficiency of retrieval rates. Moreover, the conducted experiments using multiscale energy-based feature vectors have shown the superiority of the redundant contourlet transform (RCT) for texture discrimination and retrieval, in comparison to other multiscale transforms, namely DWT, SWT, SCT and NSCT. Subsequent ongoing research directions focus on rotation invariance of such multiscale retrieval schemes.

TABLE I. AVERAGE RETRIEVAL RATES (%) IN THE TOP-15 IMAGES VS. THE NUMBER OF DECOMPOSITION LEVELS. FIVE MULTISCALE TRANSFORMS ARE COMPARED.

Transform type	2 levels		3 levels	
	Feature E_1	*Feature E_2*	*Feature E_1*	*Feature E_2*
DWT	57.68	57.84	57.43	57.95
SWT	58.13	58.35	62.96	63.54
SCT	60.78	60.56	62.96	62.89
NSCT	61.67	61.95	61.48	62.44
RCT	**63.39**	**63.54**	**64.94**	**65.16**

TABLE II. RCT AVERAGE RETRIEVAL RATES (%) COMPARED TO OTHER TRANSFORMS. RATE DIFFERENCES ARE SHOWN.

Transform type	2 levels		3 levels	
	Feature E_1	*Feature E_2*	*Feature E_1*	*Feature E_2*
RCT -DWT	+5.71	+5.70	+7.51	+7.21
RCT-SWT	+5.26	+5.19	+1.98	+1.62
RCT-SCT	+2.61	+2.98	+1.98	+2.27
RCT-NSCT	+1.72	+1.59	+3.46	+2.72
RCT	**63.39**	**63.54**	**64.94**	**65.16**

TABLE III. AVERAGE RETRIEVAL RATES (%) IN THE TOP-15 IMAGES VS. THE NUMBER OF DECOMPOSITION LEVELS. TWO REDUNDANT LAPLACIAN TRANSFORMS ARE COMPARED.

Transform type	2 levels		3 levels	
	Feature E_1	*Feature E_2*	*Feature E_1*	*Feature E_2*
NSCTLap	41.29	42.25	44.13	45.48
RCTLap	44.05	44.11	44.73	45.32
Difference	+2.76	+1.86	+0.60	-0.14

REFERENCES

[1] R. Datta, D. Joshi, J. Li, and J. Z. Wang, "Image retrieval: ideas, influences, and trends of the new age," ACM Computing Surveys 40/2:1-60, 2008.

[2] M. Mirmehdi, X. Xie, and J. Suri, Handbook of Texture Analysis. Imperial College Press, London, 2008.

[3] M. N. Do and M. Vetterli, "Wavelet-based texture retrieval using generalized Gaussian density and Kullback-Leibler distance," IEEE Trans. on Image Processing 11/2:146-158, 2002.

[4] D. Po and M. N. Do, "Directional multiscale modeling of images using the contourlet transform," IEEE Trans. on Image Processing, 15/6:1610-1620, 2006.

[5] M. S. Allili, N. Baaziz, and M. Mejri, "Texture modeling using contourlets and finite mixtures of generalized Gaussian distributions and applications," IEEE Trans. on Multimedia, 16(3), pp. 772-784, 2014.

[6] M. N. Do and M. Vetterli, "The contourlet transform: an efficient directional multiresolution image representation," IEEE Trans. on Image Processing, 14/12:2091-2106, 2005.

[7] A. L. Cunha, J. Zhou, and M. N. Do, "The nonsubsampled contourlet transform: theory, design, and applications," IEEE Trans. on Image Processing, 15/10:3089-3101, 2006.

[8] N. Baaziz, "Adaptive watermarking schemes based on a redundant contourlet transform," Proc. IEEE Int. Conf. on Image Processing (ICIP), pp. I-221-4, 2005.

[9] N. Baaziz, O. Abahmane, and R. Missaoui, "Texture feature extraction in the spatial-frequency domain for content-based image retrieval," CoRR Information Retrieval and Multimedia, arXiv:1012.5208, 2010.

[10] Vision Texture Database. [Online]. Available from: http://vismod.media.mit.edu/ pub/VisTex/ 2016.05.16

FPGA-aware Transformations of LLVM-IR

Franz Richter-Gottfried, Sebastian Hain, and Dietmar Fey
Chair of Computer Science 3 (Computer Architecture)
Friedrich-Alexander-Universität Erlangen-Nürnberg (FAU)
91058 Erlangen, Germany
email: {franz.richter-gottfried, sebastian.hain, dietmar.fey}@fau.de

Abstract—**The paper presents hardware-aware optimizations of the assembly language used by LLVM to optimize resource usage when an algorithm written in the Open Computing Language (OpenCL) is translated into a design for a field programmable gate array (FPGA) by the tool OCLAcc. In signal processing, latency and throughput of a solution are important, but also its efficiency. FPGAs offers high performance and low energy consumption for many applications, at the cost of a complex development. With high-level synthesis (HLS) the design process can be simplified significantly. We introduce our transformation of the control flow and how we minimize the bitwidth of data and operations performed. In contrast to existing work, we focus on the applicability for FPGAs and HLS from OpenCL. Both optimizations allow the generation of simpler hardware. We present metrics to rate the results with estimations of FPGA resources needed and demonstrate them using the Sobel operator, which is part of many image processing applications. Our results show that we can completely eliminate branches and reduce the total amount of bits by 16 % for a typical input configuration.**

Keywords–OpenCL; LLVM; high-level synthesis; FPGA; if-conversion; bitwidth reduction

I. INTRODUCTION

Modern FPGAs are popular for fast signal processing, because they offer a high degree of parallelism and low power consumption. This is proven, e.g., by integrated DSP blocks or hardwired floating point units on newer devices. However, it is more complex to create a custom hardware design than to optimize an algorithm for a fixed CPU. High-level synthesis (HLS) promises to fill this gap by deriving a hardware design from an algorithmic description. Inherently parallel source languages like OpenCL have the advantage that the mapping to FPGA resources is easier, compared to sequential languages like C, leading to more efficient designs. We first give a short introduction to OpenCL and the HLS-tool OCLAcc.

OpenCL: is a freely available standard created and supported by Apple, Intel and other companies. Its purpose is to describe a parallel problem and solve it on a variety of devices, managed by a host, which is usually a normal CPU. Common devices include CPUs and GPUs, but due to abstraction, host and device may even be the same physical CPU.

OpenCL defines a library interface for the host to control devices. The algorithm itself, referred to as kernel in the following, is written in the C-style language OpenCL-C. Devices offer compute units (CU), and each of them consists of processing elements (PE) to execute the kernel in parallel. Work is distributed among the PEs according to the OpenCL execution model. A work item, which is an entity in the problem space (NDRange) represents a single instance of the kernel (see Figure 1). Multiple work items share the same work group, which allows synchronization and data exchange using

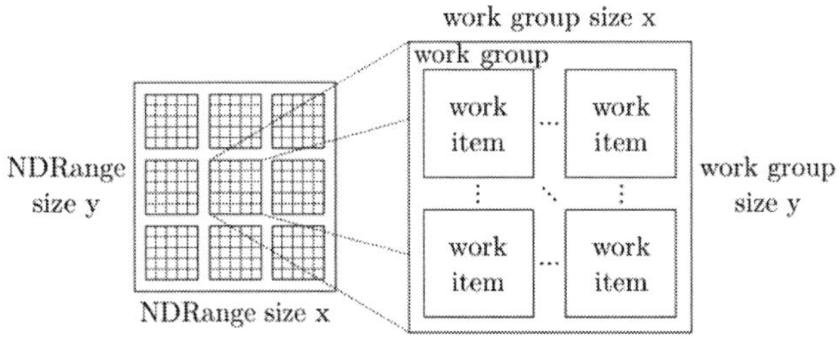

Figure 1. OpenCL Execution Model

fast local memory. In contrast, communication among work groups does not allow synchronization and relies on slower global memory, as there is no guarantee, when and on which CU work groups are scheduled.

LLVM-IR/SPIR: is a machine independent pseudo assembly language generated from the OpenCL kernel by Clang, a C-frontend for LLVM [1]. Standard Portable Intermediate Representation (SPIR) is a standardized version of LLVM-IR. Though our transformations presented target SPIR, they can also be used to optimize LLVM-IR. LLVM itself includes several passes to analyze and modify IR, e.g., alias analysis or vectorization, but most of them cannot be directly used to optimize IR for hardware generation.

OCLAcc: derives an FPGA design from OpenCL-C [2]. Figure 2 shows the steps of the transformation. Before running OCLAcc, the OpenCL kernel is translated to SPIR by a modified version of Clang maintained by the Khronos-Group. Translation in OCLAcc happens in two steps. First, SPIR is used to generate OCLAccHW, an internal representation of the data flow, optimized to derive hardware from. It works on basic blocks, which are instruction sequences always executed sequentially from the first to the last instruction. Inputs and outputs are analyzed to identify ports of the later design and streams from and to memory with their static and dynamic indices. Furthermore, the OpenCL standard includes built in functions callable by a kernel, including functions for organization, synchronization and data access, which are mapped to specific components and control inputs. OCLAccHW also is used for hardware-specific optimization. HWMap, the second step in OCLAcc, depends on the actual hardware used, i.e., vendor and type of FPGA boards. OCLAcc either directly instantiates components, generates IP-cores, or relies on inference by the vendor tools. Scheduling of components is tightly coupled with their generation, because for many parts of the system, parameters like latency or maximum clock frequency are only available when they have been implemented and cannot be used for optimization before. Instead, metrics are

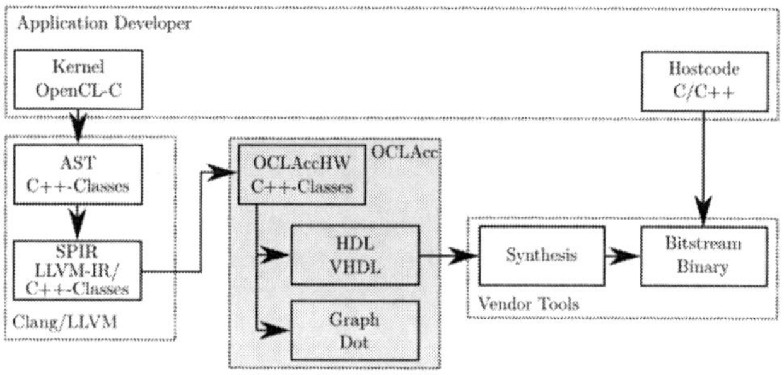

Figure 2. Components of OCLAcc

used (see Section IV). Clock synchronization of components is only done inside of basic blocks, while between blocks, each input and output carries an additional valid-bit. Blocks have to wait for their inputs to become valid before they can start computations. This minimizes synchronization overhead for the block scheduler.

Hardware generation issues: LLVM-IR is designed to be translated into code that will be executed on common CPUs or similar platforms, but an FPGA does not provide any of the capabilities of those platforms: branches cannot be directly mapped to an FPGA as there is no program counter or memory to load instructions from. Instead, the data flow defined by an instruction sequence is translated into functional units. As branches result in several basic blocks they lead to an increased synchronization overhead in form of additional registers and valid bits between those units.

OpenCL does not offer data types with variable bitwidth but only allows conventional types like `char` or `int`. In LLVM-IR and SPIR, types are mapped to integers of arbitrary bitwidth (`i1` for bool, `i32`) or floating point numbers (`float`), but Clang only uses those representing common types. This is a drawback since it is not possible to exploit the flexibility of an FPGA.

The remaining paper is structured as follows. In Section II, we present similar optimizations already published. We then introduce the example application in Section III. Sections IV and V present the transformations used to simplify the control flow and minimize the bitwidth of data paths and discuss their impact, respectively. Section VI summarizes the paper.

II. Related Work

This section gives several examples of control flow optimizations, however, most of them are designed to minimize instructions executed by a CPU. In [3] superblocks are introduced: a superblock consists of several basic blocks to enable the compiler to create code with a higher instruction level parallelism. Therefore, a sequence of basic blocks expected to be often executed forms a superblock. Then, during tail duplication, the superblock is cloned and each branch leaving and reentering the original superblock is redirected to target the cloned superblock instead. The new superblock now only has a single entry at its root to simplify scheduling inside the block and to exploit ILP. The problem for hardware generation is the process of tail duplication: copies of basic blocks increase the hardware consumption on the FPGA and have to be avoided.

The authors of [4] combine superblocks with if-conversion whereby each instruction is predicated and only executed if that condition is true. They call these blocks hyperblocks. Hyperblocks can be larger than superblocks, allowing more efficient instruction scheduling and a reduction of branches to avoid performance penalties of branching overhead and misprediction. Besides the problems of tail duplication, this approach assumes that the target architecture is able to handle predicats and can skip instructions with violated predicates. As predicates are only available at runtime, a hardware design has to implement all instructions, leading to a waste of resources.

Allen *et al.* [5] present a transformation that converts much more control flow dependencies to data flow dependencies and creates a kind of predicated execution. Branches are categorized either as forward branch, exit branch or backward branch. The first are eliminated, and during this process condition variables are introduced for each statement. If such a variable is true, the associated instruction will be executed. This simplifies the control flow graph (CFG) and control dependencies are converted into data dependencies. In [6], another algorithm for if-conversion is presented that tries to assign predicates as early as possible. Furthermore, some optimizations are presented to keep those predicates simple. Both approaches assume that predicated instructions have an advantage at runtime, which cannot be applied to hardware generation.

The authors of [7] briefly mention if-conversion for FPGAs by using multiplexers and predicates, which is in general the preferred way in hardware design. However, they do not explain or discuss when it is possible or feasible, nor do they describe the transformation in detail.

LLVM itself already provides optimization passes for if-conversion, but those work on a machine-instruction level instead of IR. This means, they operate on a hardware-specific level and depend on details of the target architecture. As OCLAcc transforms LLVM-IR code into a hardware description and does not use any machine-instructions, those optimizers cannot be used. The only integrated if-conversion optimizer working on IR-level is too conservative and does not detect all the cases of our solution.

There are also several publications explaining approaches to minimize the bitwidth of integer data paths, including software-based approaches like FRIDGE [8], which simulates the execution to get run-time values. The user constrains the range of input values to allow an interpolation of the needed bitwidth for other operations and intermediate values.

Lee *et al.* [9] present MiniBit, a static bitwidth optimizer based on range and precision analysis. Like for FRIDGE, the range of the input values is supplied by the user. Range analysis is performed with Affine Arithmetic, while they use an error function to calculate the required fraction bitwidth. The authors demonstrate the results for different algorithms on a Xilinx Virtex-4 FPGA.

Our requirements to optimize bitwidths differ from the solutions available as we only can use the information provided by the author of an OpenCL kernel, and it must not break compatibility with the OpenCL standard. We use a static approach, because it cannot be assumed that the programmer of an OpenCL kernel has run-time information.

III. Reference Code

To demonstrate our transformations, we use the Sobel operator, a simple convolution algorithm often used to preprocess

```
void kernel Sobel(global int *a, global int *b) {
    int idx = get_global_id(0), idy = get_global_id(1);
    int sx = get_global_size(0), sy = get_global_size(1);
    int v, c  = a[idy * sx + idx];
    if (idx!=0 && idx!=sx-1 && idy!=0 && idy!=sy-1) {
        int nw = a[(idy-1) * sx + idx - 1];
        int n  = a[(idy-1) * sx + idx];
        int ne = a[(idy-1) * sx + idx + 1];
        int w  = a[idy * sx + idx - 1];
        int e  = a[idy * sx + idx + 1];
        int sw = a[(idy+1) * sx + idx - 1];
        int s  = a[(idy+1) * sx + idx];
        int se = a[(idy+1) * sx + idx + 1];
        int vx = nw - ne + 2*w - 2*e + sw - se;
        int vy = nw + 2*n + ne - sw - 2*s - sw;
        v = (int) sqrt( (float)(vx*vx + vy*vy));
    } else v = c;
    b[idy * sx + idx] = v;
}
```

Figure 3. Sobel Operator

```
define cc75 void @Sobel(i32 addrspace(1)* noalias ↩
    nocapture readonly %a, i32 addrspace(1)* noalias ↩
    nocapture %b) #0 {
  %1 = tail call cc75 i32 @_Z13get_global_idj(i32 0)
  ...
  %8 = icmp eq i32 %1, 0
  br i1 %8, label %62, label %9
; <label>:9                       ; preds = %0
  ...
  %or.cond3 = or i1 %or.cond.not, %13
  br i1 %or.cond3, label %62, label %14
; <label>:14                      ; preds = %9
  ...
  br label %62
; <label>:62                      ; preds = %0, %9, %14
  %v.0 = phi i32 [ %61, %14 ], [ %7, %9 ], [ %7, %0 ]
  %63 = getelementptr i32 addrspace(1)* %b,i32 %5
  store i32 %v.0, i32 addrspace(1)* %63, align 4
  ret void
}
```

Figure 4. PHI Node Insertion

images in computer vision. It consists of two separate filter kernels, and the combination of both gives the magnitude of the gradient.

Each iteration loads eight values from memory to produce a single result. Updated values are stored in a separate image, so synchronization is only needed at the end. Since the kernel performs a single update, there is no need to explicitly synchronize at all. To update the whole image, no loop inside of the kernel is used, but instead each work item takes care of updating a single cell. Values at the border are preserved and copied into the new image. This diverging control flow is generated by an if-statement. Figure 3 shows the OpenCL kernel implementation of the Sobel operator.

Clang translates the if-statement into branches to different basic blocks, depending on which condition is met. For a CPU, this reduces the amount of instructions executed if one of the first conditions is false and the then-clause can be skipped. However, for reasonably large images, this is not the default case and the then-branch is executed far more often than the else-branch. After the if-statement, the diverged control flow is unified in IR by a PHI instruction in the last basic block. Its purpose is to select a single value from a list, depending on the block from which it was reached. This is common for single static assignment code (SSA), when the value of a variable depends on a condition, because reassigning is not allowed. See Figure 4 for the relevant parts of the generated LLVM-IR code.

IV. IF-CONVERSION

This section presents our transformations of the control flow to eliminate branches and enlarge basic blocks. To simplify the control flow, all values are computed speculatively instead of jumping to different blocks. PHI-nodes are replaced by select-instructions, which choose one of two values, depending on a condition variable.

Our transformation recognizes the if-patterns shown in Figure 5, and switch-patterns which are not covered by this paper. In all examples a condition variable is computed in the head block and evaluated by a conditional branch at its end. That branch then jumps to the proper block. After the then– or else-clause, the tail block merges the control flow again. It

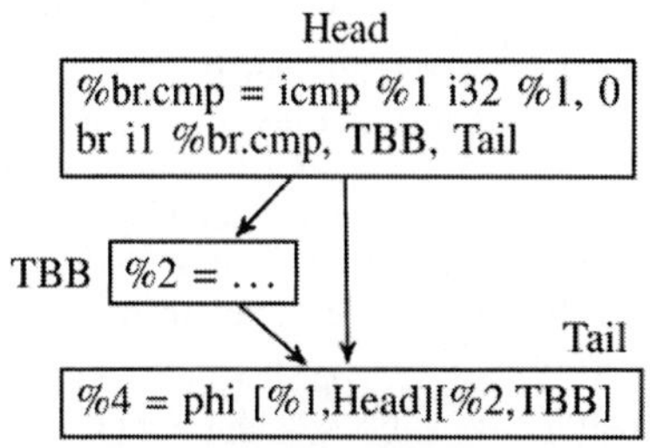

(a) Triangle for if-then

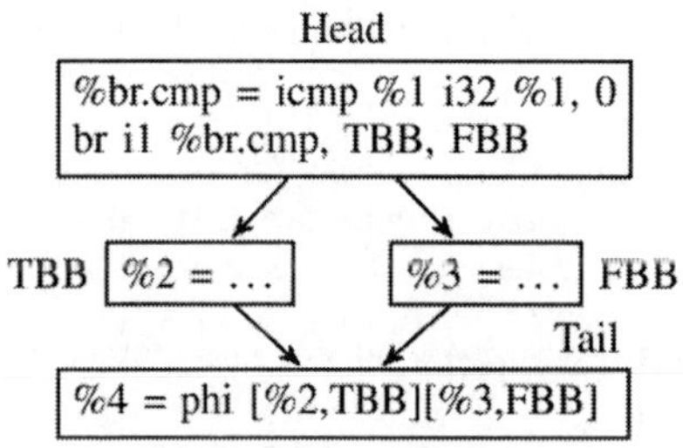

(b) Diamond for if-then-else

Figure 5. Supported patterns for if-conversion

usually contains one or more PHI-nodes to select the correct results of the branch blocks.

The goal of the transformation is to convert the shown patterns into a single basic block. Therefore, the head is merged with the branch blocks of the if-pattern (then– and else-clause) and the branch is substituted by an unconditional jump to the tail. The moved code now is always executed. It has to be ensured that the code still computes the same results, i.e., the moved instructions must not have any side-effects. Now, the PHI-nodes in the tail are adapted. Previously, they selected the results from either the then– or the else-block, depending on the if-condition. After the transformation, all possible values are defined in the head, and the PHI-nodes can be eliminated. Select-instructions are inserted to decide between the results of the then– and else-block, depending on the same condition of the former if-statement. As a final step, tail and head can be

```
define spir_func void @Sobel(i32 addrspace(1)* noalias ↩
    nocapture readonly %a, i32 addrspace(1)* noalias ↩
    nocapture %b) #0 {
  %1 = tail call spir_func i32 @_Z13get_global_idj(i32 0)
  ...
  %7 = load i32 addrspace(1)* %6, align 4
  %8 = icmp eq i32 %1, 0
  ...
  %or.cond3 = or i1 %or.cond.not, %12
  ...
  %60 = fptosi float %59 to i32
  %61 = select i1 %or.cond3, i32 %7, i32 %60
  %62 = select i1 %8, i32 %7, i32 %61
  %63 = getelementptr i32 addrspace(1)* %b, i32 %5
  store i32 %62, i32 addrspace(1)* %63, align 4
  ret void
}
```

Figure 6. Transformation of the Sobel kernel

merged into a single block and the control flow is successfully converted into a data flow using select-instructions.

Figure 6 shows the transformed Sobel kernel. All branches are eliminated and the PHI-node is replaced by two select-instructions using the conditions of the former if-statements. This also demonstrates that the transformation correctly handles nested if-patterns, because it is applied iteratively. The following section covers the implementation of the transformation in detail.

Implementation: First we find supported patterns in the CFG: they consist of the head that is always executed and that contains the compare-instructions to compute the condition of the if-statement. The condition variable is used by conditional jumps to one of the successors. Note that the head must have exactly two successors. For if-then-else-statements, the two successors are the basic blocks for then and else. We call such a pattern a diamond (Figure 5(b)). If the statement does not contain code to be executed when the condition is not met, i.e., it has no else branch, only the then-successor remains and the other one is directly the tail block. We call those patterns a triangle (Figure 5(a)). The next step in finding appropriate patterns is to investigate the branch blocks: a diamond has two branch blocks, then (TBB) and else (FBB). Both must have the head as their single predecessor and the tail as their single successor. A triangle only contains the TBB. Compiler optimizations may result in an inverted condition and thus switched TBB and FBB. This can especially be the case for negated if-conditions. Our implementation takes care of that but it is not discussed here. The final part of a pattern is the tail that merges the control flow from the branch blocks and contains the PHI-nodes that select the proper results depending on the run-time control flow. The tail may have other predecessors than the branch blocks. Successors of the tail block are irrelevant for the transformation.

If a pattern is detected, further checks have to be performed to make sure that the transformation does not change the semantics of the blocks by executing instructions with side-effects. Especially store– and synchronization-instructions are forbidden. For example, a store inside of the then-block of an if-statement may only be executed if the if-condition is true. With merging the block into head, the store-instruction is always executed, likely leading to wrong results.

As the memory-bandwidth of FPGA boards even is a stronger performance bottleneck compared to GPUs, load-instructions can be seen to have light side-effects, as we call instructions not influencing correctness but performance. By not transforming blocks with loads, performance or resource usage may also suffer as explained above, as it leads to more and shorter basic blocks. Furthermore, appropriate caches can minimize the performance penalty of speculatively executed loads. For the Sobel kernel, we do not take light side effects into account, though it is possible by the implementation. Loads are thus moved into the head and the transformed kernel consists of a single large block instead of four smaller ones. If all tests are passed, the transformation is performed. First, the instructions of the branch blocks are moved into the head, right before the final branch. The branches inside of the blocks are omitted. At this point it becomes clear, why the branch blocks must not have any other successors than the tail. Otherwise, their final instruction would be a conditional branch to reach other blocks. That branch would also have to be transferred into the head, but as branch-instructions may have side-effects they are not allowed to be executed speculatively. Therefore, the branch instruction must not be moved into the head, and as after the transformation the single successor of the head block has to be the tail block, the branch block must also have the tail as its single successor to preserve semantics.

In the next step, we determine if the tail block has other predecessors than the branch blocks. For a diamond the predecessors must include TBB and FBB. Then, the input values to the PHI-node for those two blocks are extracted. Now, as these values are moved from TBB and FBB to head, they both are already available. In those cases the usage of the operands is said to be dominated by their definitions. This also is the reason why the branch blocks must have the head as their single predecessor: instructions in the branch blocks might need operands that were computed in preceding blocks. If a branch block now has other predecessors than the head, some operands may come from those other predecessors via a PHI-node. As the branch block is now merged into the head, it is not guaranteed that the definition of the operand also dominates the head block, which means that the needed operands might not be available in the head block, leading to an invalid data flow. This issue can be solved by tail duplication as mentioned in [3] by cloning the branch block and several predecessors. The head block is modified to branch to the copied branch block and like this the branch block has the head as its single predecessor. The main disadvantage is the increased hardware consumption for the copies. Therefore, we do not convert those patterns.

Now, a select-instruction is created: input operands are the previously extracted values from the PHI-node and the condition variable is the former if-condition. The new instruction is inserted into the head block before the final branch and uses of the PHI-node are replaced by that select-instruction. The PHI-node can then be removed from the tail block. If a triangle is processed then the input values for the new select-instruction come from the head block (if the if-condition is false) and the block for the then-part. The other steps are equal to those of processing a diamond. After the transformation, PHI-nodes in the tail are eliminated.

If the tail block has other predecessors than the branch blocks, the PHI-node cannot be eliminated. As the tail block can be reached via other control paths that do not contain

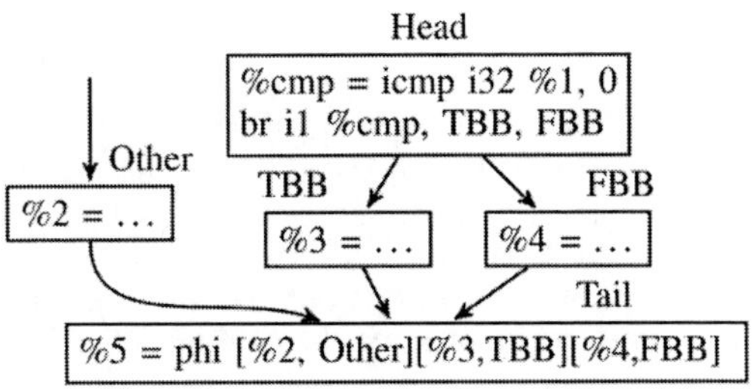

(a) Original

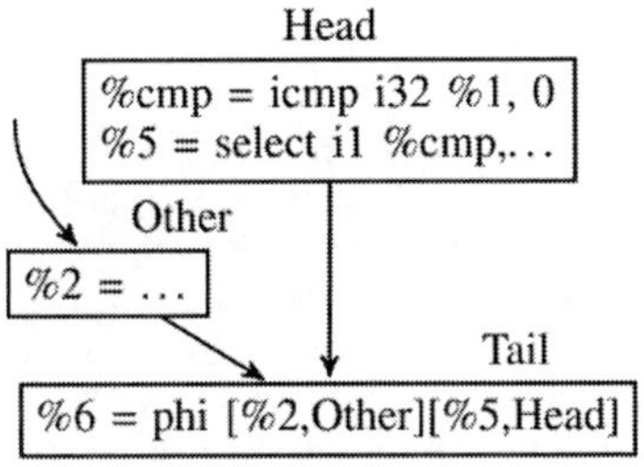

(b) Transformed

Figure 7. Control Flow Transformation of Diamond Pattern

the if-statement, the PHI-nodes have input values for other blocks as well. As a select instruction would just be able to choose between the values from the two paths of the currently processed if-statement, the PHI-node is still needed to choose between that preselected value and those values for the other predecessors not under control of the processed if-statement. This is the case for a nested if-statement. Nevertheless, in this case, the number of input values to the PHI-node can be reduced.

In a last step, the final branch of the head is replaced by an unconditional branch to the tail. It is tested if the tail can be merged into the head block: if the tail has the head as its single predecessor, head and tail can be merged, which eliminates the branch.

Figure 7(a) shows a diamond, where the PHI-nodes cannot be completely replaced. During the transformation the code from TBB and FBB is merged into the head block. Then, for each PHI-node in the tail block, a select instruction is created with the former if-condition (`%cmp`). The input values for the select instruction are extracted from the PHI-node. But as the tail block has other predecessors than TBB and FBB, the PHI-node cannot be replaced (Figure 7(b)).

The transformation is repeated until no more patterns are found. By that, nested if-statements can also be converted. Figure 8 shows the CFG corresponding to Figure 3 containing two triangles: the first triangle consists of BB9 as head, BB62 as tail and BB14 as branch. BB14 is merged into BB9 in the way described above: a select-instruction is inserted into BB62 to either select `%7` or `%60` depending on the value of `%or.cond3`. As BB62 has other predecessors than BB9 and BB14, the PHI-node is not removed but the input operands for BB9 and BB14 are replaced by the result of the created select instruction (the result is stored in `%61`). Now the next triangle gets visible consisting of the entry block, BB62 as tail and the merged block BB9/BB14. This new pattern can

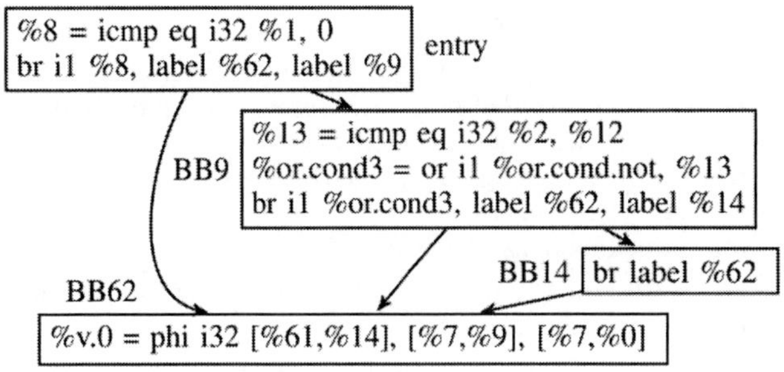

Figure 8. CFG of Sobel

now be transformed, too: again a select instruction is inserted using the new input values of the PHI-node: `%7` and `%61`. As condition variable `%8` (defined in the entry block) is used. But as now the PHI-node does not have any other predecessors than BB9/BB14 and entry, it can be removed and all instructions using its result will use the result of this second select. Finally, Figure 6 shows the fully transformed code using the created select-instructions.

Metrics: The implementation is able to consider certain additional soft constraints. Those are used to determine whether the transformation is useful to reduce hardware resources. Currently, the block size can be used to prevent the transformation to take place. This is useful if the critical path of the new block is very long. As one block can execute a single work item, a long critical path may degrade performance. More elaborate metrics take FPGA resources like LUTs, registers and BlockRAM into account.

A first indicator for those numbers is the amount of instructions in a block. All instructions are weighted equally, ignoring their operation or number and size of their operands. This of course is only a very rough estimation, but it can be computed very fast and it does not need any knowledge of the target device. For the Sobel kernel, we can replace four basic blocks with 72 instructions in total and different length to a single block with only 70 instructions. On the other hand, if the current kernel computes a border value, the same work has to be done instead of only 13 instructions.

To take the differing complexity of operations into account, instructions can be weighted by an instruction-specific factor. A bitwise shift operation is far cheaper than a division, represented by a smaller coefficient. Furthermore, number and size of operands give an additional weight.

More accurate metrics need knowledge of the targeted FPGA. Depending on the available resources, instructions can be mapped to different hardware, e.g., DSP blocks or IP cores. Prototypes of the instructions are synthesized by the backend of OCLAcc and the results of the vendor tools give the hardware consumption. This gives the most precise estimation of the resources needed. In fact, it even overestimates them as global hardware optimizations performed by the synthesis tool are not available when each component is separately synthesized. However, the estimation may take a very long time.

V. Minimize Bitwidth

As already mentioned, OpenCL does not support custom data types, which is one of the key advantages of an FPGA design. This cannot be circumvented by adding keywords to the OpenCL frontend, because this would invalidate the kernel for other OpenCL platforms. The optimization presented works for integer values, which of course may also be a fixed point representation. This is often used in hardware design to save resources for integer but not for floating point values, because of the requirements of IEEE 754.

Similar to Altera's SDK for OpenCL, our transformation requires user input to statically reduce bitwidths in the form of bitmasks applied to variables. Typically, constrains are set for inputs and output, and all operations and values in between are derived from them. For the example in Figure 3, each load from image `a` may be replaced with `0xFFFFFF & a[...]` if only 3 Byte per pixel are to be processed. Constant values, which have no dedicated bitwidth in LLVM-IR, are stored with the minimum of bits. Though these optimizations may seem trivial, many cases have to be respected as explained in the following.

Implementation: We have to differentiate between values and constants. A value, starting with a % in LLVM-IR, has a fixed type (`i32` for 32 bit integer, `float`), but integer values are signless. However, a constant (`true`, `-1`, `1.5`) does not have a fixed bitwidth but it depends on the type of the operation using it, e.g., `%29 = add nsw i32 %5, -1` assigns the sum of value `%5` and the constant `-1` to `%29` without declaring the constant's bitwidth.

For values and constant operands, the bitwidth of the type and the minimum bitwidth are stored, as well as flags to indicate whether no extension (next), sign-extension (sext), zero-extension (zext) or one-extension (oext) has to be used. To gather the minimum bitwidth, the transformation is split into two phases: a forward propagation (FP) for each value, starting at the first instruction of the first basic block to get the minimum based on input width and the operation and a backward propagation (BP) in reverse to determine the actual bitwidth used, depending on the output.

In the forward step, we predict the required bitwidth based on its operands. If there is at least one zext operand, the output is as wide as the smallest of them. This is safe since all leading zeros of the operand eliminate possible ones of others, independent of their length. If all inputs are sext the required bitwidth is as wide as the output's width because sign-bits cannot be determined statically. For example, if all sign-bits of the operands are one, the result also is one-extended. On the other hand, we cannot just use the sext-flag as one input may be positive with a zero sign-bit, resulting in an output value being zero from that bit on.

For BP, we start with the bitwidth from FP. If any of the instruction's operands is a constant, its width delimits the instruction's, and all other operands' bitwidth. This is true even if FP resulted in a wider operation. If we have no requirements from FP, we use the width of the smallest operand to be propagated to it's predecessors.

In general, the bitwidth of constants can only be determined based on an operation using it. The constant -1 can be encoded using a single bit in two's complement, which works with signed operations like integer multiplication. For bitwise operations and operations being the same operation for signed and unsigned values (e.g., add), its width has to fit the other operands' to prevent wrong results.

By these steps, we first learn how wide a value may become because of the operations performed to compute it, and then reduce its size to a minimum based on the width of its users.

Results: The exact number of bits saved depends on the application, precisely the exact width of input and output values. The results demonstrate the effects of our optimization for the Sobel operator, but will be different for other applications. For the kernel in Figure 3, we save 414 bits of 2528 or around 16% for operations and 496 bits for constants if we limit input and output to 24 bit by using bitmasks, and the complexity of operations and thus the resource usage on an FPGA is significantly reduced.

VI. Conclusion

In this paper, we presented an algorithm to simplify the control flow of a given OpenCL kernel by transforming several blocks of if– or switch-statements into a single basic block. The new block's instructions coming from different branches are executed speculatively and the correct value is chosen depending on the if-condition by a select-instruction. We also presented a static method to reduce the bitwidth of instructions and constants, based on user-provided bitmasks. Both enable OCLAcc to produce more efficient and less complex hardware designs, inevitable for fast and efficient FPGA designs of signal processing applications.

References

[1] C. Lattner and V. Adve, "LLVM: A compilation framework for lifelong program analysis and transformation," San Jose, CA, USA, Mar 2004, pp. 75–88.

[2] F. Richter-Gottfried and D. Fey, "OCLAcc: An open-source generator for configurable logic block based accelerators," in Embedded World Conference Proceedings, Feb 2014.

[3] W. M. W. Hwu et al., "The superblock: An effective technique for vliw and superscalar compilation," The Journal of Supercomputing, vol. 7, no. 1, pp. 229–248.

[4] S. A. Mahlke, D. C. Lin, W. Y. Chen, R. E. Hank, and R. A. Bringmann, "Effective compiler support for predicated execution using the hyperblock," SIGMICRO Newsl., vol. 23, no. 1-2, Dec. 1992, pp. 45–54.

[5] J. R. Allen, K. Kennedy, C. Porterfield, and J. Warren, "Conversion of control dependence to data dependence," in Proceedings of the 10th ACM SIGACT-SIGPLAN Symposium on Principles of Programming Languages, ser. POPL '83. New York, NY, USA: ACM, 1983, pp. 177–189.

[6] J. Z. Fang, "Compiler algorithms on if-conversion, speculative predicates assignment and predicated code optimizations," in Proceedings of the 9th International Workshop on Languages and Compilers for Parallel Computing, ser. LCPC '96. London, UK, UK: Springer-Verlag, 1997, pp. 135–153.

[7] S. Hauck and A. DeHon, Reconfigurable Computing: The Theory and Practice of FPGA-Based Computation. San Francisco, CA, USA: Morgan Kaufmann Publishers Inc., 2007, pp. 158–159.

[8] M. Willems, V. Bursgens, T. Grotker, and H. Meyr, "Fridge: an interactive code generation environment for hw/sw codesign," in Acoustics, Speech, and Signal Processing, 1997. ICASSP-97., 1997 IEEE International Conference on, vol. 1, Apr 1997, pp. 287–290 vol.1.

[9] D. Lee et al., "Accuracy-guaranteed bit-width optimization," IEEE Trans. on CAD of Integrated Circuits and Systems, vol. 25, no. 10, 2006, pp. 1990–2000. [Online]. Available: http://dx.doi.org/10.1109/TCAD.2006.873887

Automatic Elimination of High Amplitude Artifacts in EEG Signals

Ana Rita Teixeira
University of Aveiro / IEETA IPC/ ESEC
3810 Aveiro, Portugal
Email: ateixeira@ua.pt

Ana Maria Tomé
University of Aveiro / IEETA
3810 Aveiro, Portugal
Email: ana@ieeta.pt

Isabel Maria Santos
University of Aveiro / CINTESIS
3810 Aveiro, Portugal
Email: isabel.santos@ua.pt

Abstract—**High amplitude artifacts represent a problem during EEG recordings in neuroscience research. Taking this into account, this paper proposes a method to identify high amplitude artifacts with no requirement for visual inspection, electrooculogram (EOG) reference channel or user assigned parameters. A potential solution to the high amplitude artifacts (HAA) elimination is presented based on the blind source separation technique. The assumption underlying the selection of components is that HAA are independent of the EEG signal and different HAA can be generated during the EEG recordings. Therefore, the number of components related to HAA is variable and depends on the processed signal, which means that the method is adaptable to the input signal. The results demonstrate that the proposed method preferably removes the signal associated to the delta band and maintains the EEG signal information in other bands with a high relative precision, thus improving the quality of the EEG signal. A case study with EEG signals obtained during performance on the Halstead Category Test (HCT) is presented. After HAA removal, data analysis revealed an error-related frontal ERP wave: the feedback-related negativity (FRN) in response to feedback stimuli.**

Keywords–BSS; EEG; ERP; Source Selection

I. Introduction

The electroencephalogram (EEG) signals measured by placing electrodes over the scalp represent the bioelectrical brain activity which may be used, amongst different applications, in neuroscience studies. During the recordings, the EEG signal is, unfortunately, often contaminated with different physiological factors independent of the cerebral activity, which are typically not of interest - assigned artifacts. The artifacts elimination is an important issue in EEG signal processing and is in many studies a prerequisite for the subsequent signal analysis. In many applications, such as brain computer interface (BCI), the features of the EEG signals are used as a command to control devices and the presence of such artifacts can degrade the performance of the system.

There are several EEG waveforms that differ from background EEG rhythms and may be of interest for particular research and clinical assessment aims. A relevant type of waveform that is studied independently from background EEG activity is the event-related potential (ERP). ERPs are deterministic signals, i.e., they are elicited by specific stimuli or events, and not spontaneous like the rhythms, being a transient form of brain activity generated in the brain structures.
Recent studies show that ERP waves can be used for non-muscular BCI control. There are advantages and drawbacks of using ERPs in BCI. The two main advantages are that 1) ERPs are naturally occuring brain responses, which the user produces without any particular training; 2) ERPs occur at short latencies, which is a beneficial property for the throughput of a BCI. However, these advantages are counterbalanced by some drawbacks. Firstly there are large inter-individual differences in ERP latencies and waveforms, requiring the system to be trained to recognize the ERP of a given individual. Another drawback is that ERP waves have so small amplitudes and are dominated by background activity, that makes them difficult to detect to the human eye. Several methods exist to extract the ERP signal from the EEG background. Simple signal processing techniques including averaging over consecutive trials can reveal their shape and allow their analysis if the EEG signal is not corrupted by artifacts, mainly high amplitude artifacts.
The high amplitude artifacts that derive from eye blinking, eye movements and patient movements affect the scalp EEG channels differently. The frontal scalp channels are impacted the most by these kinds of artifacts. Furthermore, these artifacts have a more significant impact on the temporal correlation with frontal scalp signals than the remaining channels. The high amplitude artifact correction can be regarded as a preprocessing method to clean the EEG signal. There are three main ways of dealing with high amplitude artifacts.

1) Prevention:
Minimize the occurrence of ocular artifacts and patient movements by giving proper instructions to participants. However the ocular artifacts are spontaneous and involuntary, so this is often unavoidable.
2) Epoch Rejection - Manual Method:
This is a very simple method to eliminate the artifacts in EEG signals. If an artifact exists in an epoch, then the corrupted epoch is removed. Important data will be lost during the removal process, particularly when limited amount of data is available or when a lot of artifacts exist in EEG signals.
3) Elimination of artifacts:
Different denoising techniques can be used to eliminate artifacts from the EEG signal. This is the best approach for cleaning the EEG because the number of epochs is preserved.

Techniques of Blind Source Separation (BSS) like Independent Components Analysis (ICA) are promising approaches to decompose the EEG signal in independent components able to identify the artifacts. Although there are several proposals in the literature for an automatic selection of components, all of which require free input parameters, a visual inspection by the user or the EOG reference signal is needed.

The methods used to reject sources with high amplitude can be highlighted: with sparsity greater than some threshold [1], [2], the extreme values in amplitude, the probability measure using the kurtosis value [3], the mutual information and the spectral pattern [1]. In [1], a subsystem to identify artefactual sources is used based in computing ten statistical measures. These measures are computed for each source and some of them involve the EOG signal reference. In [4], a method to find the ICs representing the muscle artifacts is described. The ICs are classified in a descending order according to their respective auto-correlation values and afterwards some decisions to reject sources are made. As the auto-correlation of muscle artifacts is relatively low with respect to that of the EEG signal, the ICs representing the muscle artifacts are expected to be among the last components. In [5] each IC derived by SOBI is then band-pass filtered between $1-10$ Hz to create filtered ICs. The Pearson correlation is calculated between the ICs filtered and the accelerometer signal and a threshold is used to eliminate the components with high correlation value. Different EEGLAB plug-ins were also developed to automatic select the artifact components, such as ADJUST [6], FASTER [7] and AAR [3] based in source probability and in kurtosis values.

The component selection based in the correlation based index (CBI) described in [8] and based in radial frontocentral topographic scalp distribution [9] is used in this study. Such approach is able to identify high amplitude artifacts in a fully automatic way without requiring visual inspection, the EOG reference channel or free parameters as input. This study presents a potential solution to the high amplitude artifacts (HAA) elimination. The assumption underlying the selection method is that HAA are independent of the EEG signal and different HAA can be generated during the EEG recordings. Therefore, the number of components related to HAA is variable and dependent on the processed signal, which means that the method is adaptive to the signal. The proposed method reduces the influence of high amplitude artifacts and improves the quality of the EEG allowing to find different ERP waves.

A study case with the Halstead Category Test (HCT) [10] is presented in this paper. Based on the literature, the aim is to find larger negative amplitudes measured maximally at midline fronto-central electrodes - the feedback-related negativity (FRN) wave [11]. The FRN occurs when the feedback does not conform to the user's expectations after the feedback stimuli. It has been established for years that the brain produces specific evoked responses in case of errors. Along that line, a couple of recent studies have proposed to use error-related brain signals in BCI applications [12]. The use of Error Potentials in BCI arises from the observation that this additional information provided automatically by the user could be used to improve the BCI performance, [13]. The results demonstrate the existence of EEG activity recorded in central scalp locations that is related to error processing, namely the FRN. Specifically, the preprocessing data analysis described revealed an FRN wave during performance on the HCT, a well-established neuropsychological measure of non-verbal reasoning, abstract concept formation and cognitive flexibility, which are aspects of the cognitive executive function. Therefore, this preprocessing method shows potential to be used in improving the quality of the EEG signal used in neuroscience studies. In particular, the results can be useful in BCI applications to clean high amplitude artifacts as well as in detection of FRN waves.

This paper is organized as follows. In section II, the blind source separation technique is described and in section III, the new source selection methodology is presented. The experimental procedure is described in section IV and some metrics for algorithm validations are discussed in section V. Finally, results and conclusions are presented in section VI and VII, respectively.

II. Blind Source Separation

The effectiveness of the BSS technique depends on some assumptions, according to the studied problem, such as: independence, linearity, uncorrelatedness, non-gaussianity, among others described in the literature. The more closely the hypotheses advanced by a certain algorithm are satisfied, the better the method is meant to separate the components. Success hence critically depends on good source separation and on correct identification of sources as brain activity or artifact components. In the literature, BSS is considered to be the best approach for artifacts of high signal to noise ratio (SNR), i.e., high amplitude artifacts [14]. Linear Blind Source Separation models can be expressed algebraically as

$$\mathbf{X} = \mathbf{AS} \tag{1}$$

where the sensored EEG data is organized into a $C \times N$ matrix $\mathbf{X}$, representing C the number of channels and N the number of time points; $\mathbf{A}$ is the $C \times C$ mixing matrix and $\mathbf{S}$ is a $C \times N$ matrix of unknown sources or independent components. The goal of BSS or ICA algorithms is to determine the sources and the separation matrix $\mathbf{B}$ given the measured/ sensored signals $\mathbf{X}$. So, the separation equation reads

$$\mathbf{S} = \mathbf{BX} \tag{2}$$

where $\mathbf{B}$ can be defined as the pseudo-inverse of the mixing matrix, i.e., $\mathbf{B} = \mathbf{A}^{\dagger}$.

Most of BSS/ICA algorithms follow a two step procedure to estimate the separation (or de-mixing) matrix [4]. The first step is based on Principal Component Analysis or Singular Value Decomposition (SVD) of the data matrix $\mathbf{X}$ [15]. For the second step different approaches have been proposed [15]. The separation matrix $\mathbf{B}$ is estimated as the product of matrices computed in both steps. For convenience, these steps are reviewed for the Second Order Blind Identification (SOBI) [16].

- With the SVD of the original data $\mathbf{X}$, two $C \times C$ matrices are computed: the eigenvector matrix $\mathbf{V}$ and the diagonal singular value matrix $\mathbf{D}$. Note that a dimension reduction can be performed by reducing the number of singular values and eigenvectors in the corresponding matrices.
- After whitening the original data, i.e., $\mathbf{Z} = \mathbf{D}^{-1}\mathbf{V}^T\mathbf{X}$, L time-delayed correlation matrices are estimated. The approximate join diagonalization of these set of matrices gives an orthogonal matrix $\mathbf{U}$.

The separation matrix is defined as $\mathbf{B} = \mathbf{U}^T\mathbf{D}^{-1}\mathbf{V}^T$ and its pseudo-inverse as $\mathbf{A} = \mathbf{VDU}$. The mandatory parameter of this algorithm is L, the number of matrices of second step. Eventually, the user can decide to perform dimension reduction after the first step by discarding the smallest singular values and corresponding eigenvectors. In this work, the dimension was maintained equal to the number of sensors (channels), i. e. C, and the L is assigned to 100 and the default value of the energy of the components, i.e., the rows of the matrix

S, is equal to one. Therefore, the coefficients of the mixing matrix can be used to decide the relevance of the sources in the respective linearly mixed signal.

III. Source Selection

Source selection, in BSS applications, is the most widely problem reported in the literature [4]. Existing methods for artifact rejection can be separated into hand-optimized, semi-automatic and fully automatic approaches. Semi-automatic approaches require user interaction for ambiguous or outlier components, while fully automated methods were proposed for the classification of artifacts. Whatever is the case, different metrics have been applied directly to the mixing matrix $\mathbf{A}$ or to the sources $\mathbf{S}$ in order to select artifact related components. In this study, as the sources have energy one, the columns of the mixing matrix determines the power distribution of the reconstructed sources over scalp. Given, the mixing matrix $\mathbf{A}$

$$\mathbf{A} = \begin{pmatrix} a_{11} & a_{12} & \dots & a_{1C} \\ a_{21} & a_{22} & \dots & a_{2C} \\ \dots & \dots & & \dots \\ a_{C1} & a_{C2} & \dots & a_{CC} \end{pmatrix} \quad (3)$$

where a_{ij}, $(1 \leq i, j \leq C)$ is the transfer coefficient from $j-th$ source to the $i-th$ observed channel signal. Each column vector of the matrix $\mathbf{A}$ reflects the power propagating across all scalp channels of the corresponding row of $\mathbf{S}$ (one source). In this work it is proposed a two-step fully automatic source selection procedure. The first step measures the influence, over all scalp, of each source by estimating the following coefficient

$$CBI(j) = \sum_{i=1}^{C} \frac{|a_{ij}|}{\sqrt{a_{i1}^2 + a_{i2}^2 + \dots + a_{iC}^2}} \quad (4)$$

Experimentally it was verified that the plot of CBI values, ordered by decreasing order of magnitude, shows an abrupt decrease on the first five values and then stabilizes. So, the five largest CBI values are initially identified as candidate columns of the matrix $\mathbf{A}$ associated to the high amplitude artifacts. For the sake of simplicity, from now on assume that the columns of $\mathbf{A}$ and the rows of $\mathbf{S}$ are ordered according to the values of the coefficient CBI. Re-writing the mixing model as a sum of outer products

$$\tilde{\mathbf{X}} = \mathbf{AS} = \mathbf{A}_{*1}\mathbf{S}_{1*} + \mathbf{A}_{*2}\mathbf{S}_{2*} + \ldots + \mathbf{A}_{*C}\mathbf{S}_{C*} \quad (5)$$

where the first term on the right side of the equation 5 corresponds to the source spreading, over the scalp,with largest energy; the second term corresponds to the source spreading with the second largest energy and so on. As referred before, the graphical representation the columns of $\mathbf{A}$ is often used by experts to identify visually the artifacts. The second step of the selection procedure is an application of one of the rules used in this context. To find out if a certain source is an artifact related component it is foreseen that it contributes mostly in the frontal region. To confirm if the five selected candidate columns with highest CBI are related to the high amplitude artifact, the power distribution for all selected j columns should verify the condition $|a_{ij} > |a_{kj}|$, $\forall i \in L_1$ and $k \in L_2$ where $L_1 = [Fp1; Fpz; FP2]$ and $L_2 = [F7; F3; Fz; F4; F8]$ Note after the selection of the artefact related sources the original signal is decomposed into the artefact related signal and the clean signal. The reconstructed signal is then obtained without high amplitude artifacts. By the explanation above it is clear that the EEG signal can be expressed as:

$$\mathbf{X} = (\mathbf{A_1} + \mathbf{A_2})\mathbf{S} \quad (6)$$

where $\mathbf{A_1}$ $(C \times C)$ is the matrix with columns associated to the EEG activity (Clean Data) and $\mathbf{A_2}$ $(C \times C)$ is the matrix with $j \leq 5$ non null columns associated to the high amplitude artifacts activity (HAA Data).

IV. Experimental procedure

A. Participants and Task

Fifty eight EEG signals belonging to 58 participants with 208 trials each were collected with a Neuroscan SynAmps2 amplifier through an Easy-Cap with 26 channels and recorded with the software Scan 4.3 (Neuroscan Systems). EEG was continuously recorded with Ag-AgCl sintered electrodes which were located according to the $10-20$ system. A computerized version of the Halstead Category Test (HCT) was used to assess cognitive executive frontal lobe function. This test is used to measure a person's ability to formulate abstract principles based on receiving feedback after each specific test item. Visual feedback is provided after each trial, to indicate if the participant responded wrong or right.

B. Dataset

For signal analysis, each EEG trial was epoched from 6000 ms prior to response onset to 3000 ms after, leading to a dataset with 208 trials for each of the 58 participants. Note that after 1500 ms of response onset the feedback was provided and the dataset for each participant can be divided considering the conditions wrong and right.

In this study, the Raw Data signal is the filtered EEG between $[1-40]$ Hz in frequency, trial by trial, for each participant; the Clean Data signal is the processed Raw Data by SOBI algorithm with full automatic criteria to select the sources associated with the high amplitude artifacts; and the HAA Data is the reconstructed signal with the automatically rejected sources.

C. Algorithm Performance

As mentioned above, the SOBI algorithm is employed to decompose all epochs into two datasets: Clean and HAA Data. The selection of components is fully automatic, adaptable to each epoch allowing the identification of HAA signal. The number of selected components is variable between 0 and 5. Although almost all epochs in the present dataset were corrupted with high amplitude artifacts, there were occasionally epochs without artifact. In epochs without artifacts, no components are selected. In these datasets $\approx$ 97% of the trials were corrupted with artifacts and the number of selected components in all trials ranged in average between 1.85 ± 0.98. To demonstrate the algorithm performance two distinct cases are discussed: Case 1 - An epoch without artifacts and Case 2 - An epoch with artifacts.

- **Case 1: Epoch without artifact** Figure 1 (a) represents an example of an epoch without artifact (only 1 second is represented). In this case, the algorithm did not select any component. Considering the maximum peak of the channel $Fp1$, an average head topography centered in the 100 ms window around the peak was constructed, Figure 1 (b), to illustrate that there are no high-amplitude components in this epoch.

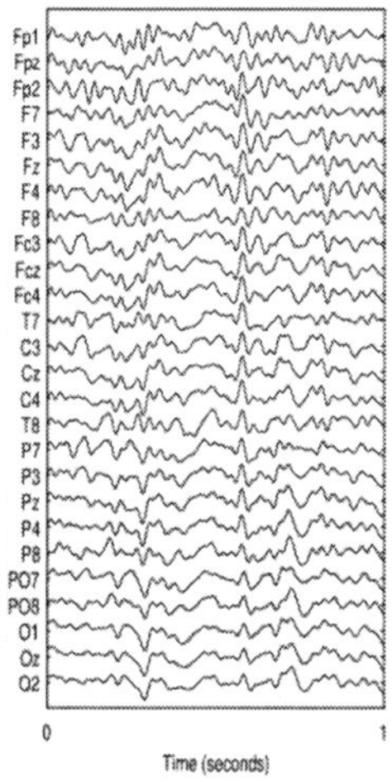

(a) Raw Data

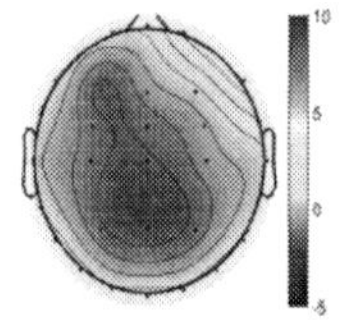

(b) Topogram of the Raw Data

Figure 1. Case 1: (a) Original Epoch - Raw Data (b) Head topography of the corresponding Raw Data considering an average window of 100 ms centered in maximum peak of the $Fp1$ channel.

- **Case 2: Epoch with artifact** In Figure 2 (a) is represented an example of an epoch with an artifact (only 1 second is represented) . In this case, the algorithm selected 4 components (S_{*1}, S_{*3}, S_{*4} and S_{*5}) of the 5 with the largest spread on the scalp. As shown in the head topographies, Figure 2 (d), all components selected by the algorithm have a strong power energy in frontal channels. It should be noted that, although the first component has the highest energy in the frontal channels, the selection is not sufficient to remove the HAA signal, as described in [8] .

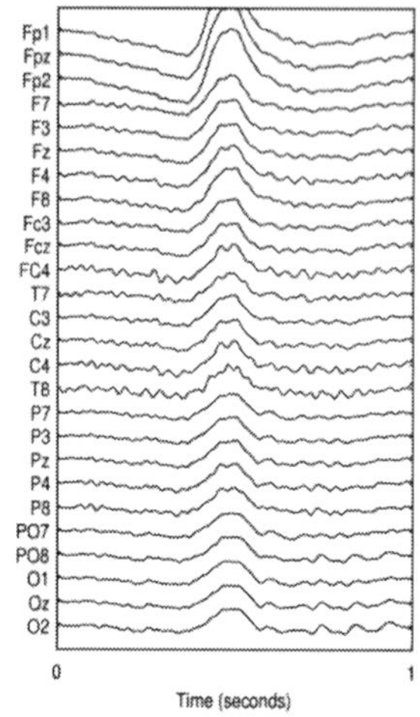

(a) Raw Data

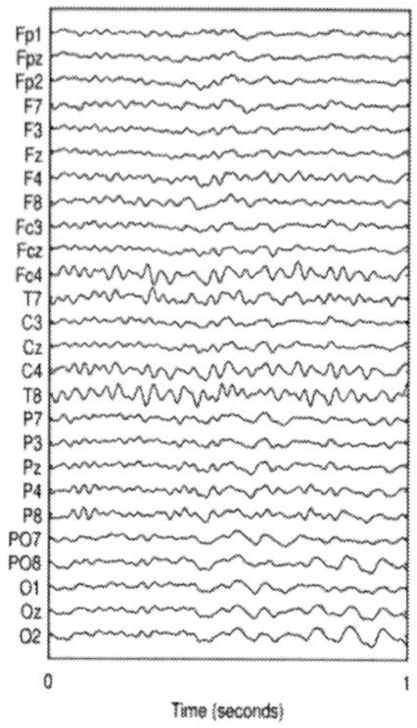

(b) Clean Data

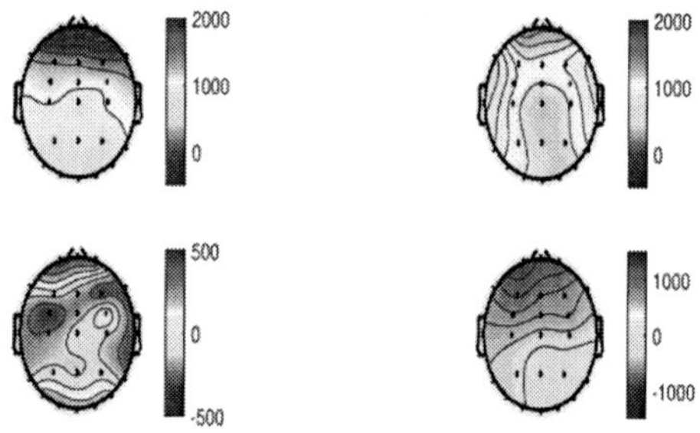

(c) Topograms of the selected IC's.

Figure 2. Case2: (a) Original Epoch - Raw Data (b) Clean Data after HAA signal removed by the automatic proposed method to select the ICs (c) Independent Components obtained by SOBI algorithm (d) Head topography of the selected ICs associated to HAA signal.

V. Metrics for Algorithm Validation

The efficiency of the automatic method of selection of components was validated using different metrics to compare the Raw Data, the Clean Data and the HAA Data in time and frequency domains in each epoch for all participants. Firstly, the datasets (Raw, Clean and HAA signals) were grouped according to the region of the scalp where the electrodes are located. To account for spatial differences in amplitude distribution, channels were grouped into 6 regions, $R1$: prefrontal channels $(Fp1, Fp2, Fpz)$, $R2$: frontal channels $(F7, F3, Fz, F4, F8)$, $R3$: frontocentral channels $(FC3, FCz, FC4, C3, Cz, C4)$, $R4$: parietal channels $(P7, P3, Pz, P4, P8)$, $R5$: parieto-occipital channels $(PO7, PO8, O1, Oz, O2)$ and $R6$: temporal channels $(T7, T8)$.

The three datasets in each region $(R1-R6)$ were band-pass filtered ($6th$ order Butterworth) , with a zero-phase strategy, into delta: $[1 \;\; 4]$ Hz; theta: $[4 \;\; 7]$ Hz; alpha: $[7 \;\; 13]$ Hz and beta: $[13 \;\; 30]$ frequency bands. For all epochs and for all participants, the following metrics were then calculated per band in each region and were performed in three ways: (1) correlation coefficient in time for all signals between: Clean/Raw data; Clean/HAA Data; Raw/HAA Data; (2) coherence of average signal between Clean/Raw Data and Raw/HAA Data and (3) Mean Power to compute relative power between the Clean and Raw Data.

The correlation coefficient was calculated between the Clean/Raw Data, the Clean/HAA Data and the Raw/HAA Data for all bands in all regions, but only region $R5$ is represented in Figure 3. The results show that the Clean/Raw Data has an high correlation in beta, alpha and theta bands and, in turn, Raw/HAA Data presents high correlation in the delta band. Thus, the proposed method reduces the influence of signals associated to the delta band. Figure 4 presents the results

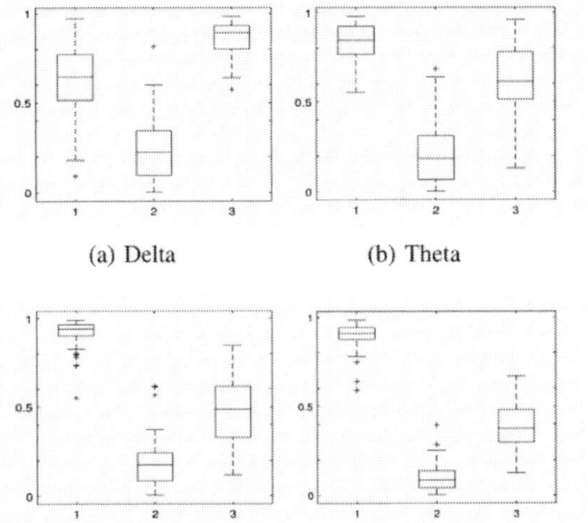

(a) Delta (b) Theta

(c) Alpha (d) Beta

Figure 3. Correlation Coefficient between (1) - Clean/Raw Data ; (2) - Clean/HAA Data ; (3) - Raw/HAA Data in each band for region $R5$

of the computation of the coherence magnitude between the Raw/Clean Data and Raw/HAA Data in regions $R3$ and $R5$. Region $R5$ is less corrupted with artifacts than region $R3$ and because of this the main difference between the results is in delta band values, where the coherence is less than 0.5 in region $R3$ and over 0.5 in region $R5$. In the theta, alpha and beta bands the coherence value for the two datasets is similar in the two regions. These results confirm that the selected components are correlated to the delta bandwidth by ensuring that the remaining frequency bands are unaffected, especially alpha and beta bands. To measure the relation in each band

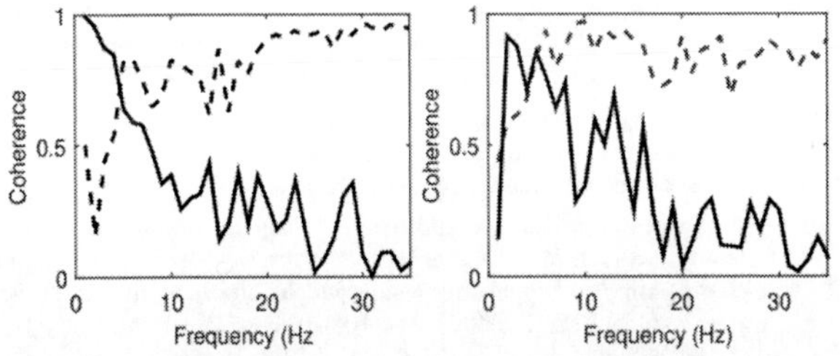

(a) R3 (b) R5

Figure 4. Coherence Magnitude in $R3$ (a) and $R5$ (b) region between the Raw/Clean Data (dash line) and between Raw/HAA Data (solid line).

between the Clean and Raw Data, the relative energy power (RP) for each region was computed as:

$$RP = \frac{\sum_{i=1}^{58} \sum_{n=1}^{9000} x_{c_i}(n)^2}{\sum_{i=1}^{58} \sum_{n=1}^{9000} x_{ri}(n)^2} \quad (7)$$

where x_{c_i} is the Clean Data and x_{r_i} is the Raw Data in each band computed for each region and for all participants $i = 1 : 58$. The results are consistent with the results described above considering the different metrics. The relative power between Clean/Raw Data in region $R3$ is presented in Figure 5. Once again, it can be seen that the band with greater loss of information is the delta band with some 40% and that the alpha and beta bands exhibit residual losses, $\approx 10\%$.

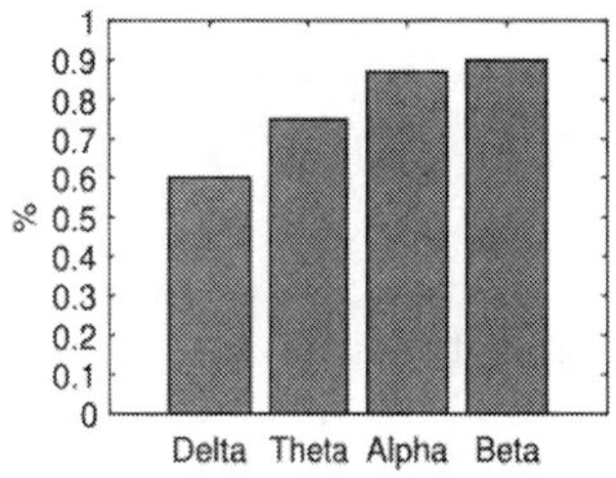

Figure 5. Relative Power between Clean/Raw Data in region $R3$.

VI. Event-Related Potentials

The aim of the current study was to show a new automatic selection algorithm for ICA decompositions to remove high amplitude artifacts in EEG signals. The data used in this study was highly corrupted with artifacts and hence compromises the interpretation of many psychophysiological correlates. In this particular case, the detection of ERP waves associated to performance in the HCT was nearly impossible. To show the impact of the application of this method and its ability to clean the high amplitude artifacts in the signal, the grand average signal of all participants in an average window between $[200 \quad 300]$ ms after the feedback is used, this is depicted in Figure 6 (a). The grand average of the HAA and Clean Data in the same window is also considered, Figures 6 (b) and (c), respectively. The head topographies of the raw data show an high amplitude signal in the frontal channels that mask any ERP wave present. After applying the SOBI algorithm and the automatic component selection, the Clean Data presents a negativity in the central area, that is not evident in the Raw data.

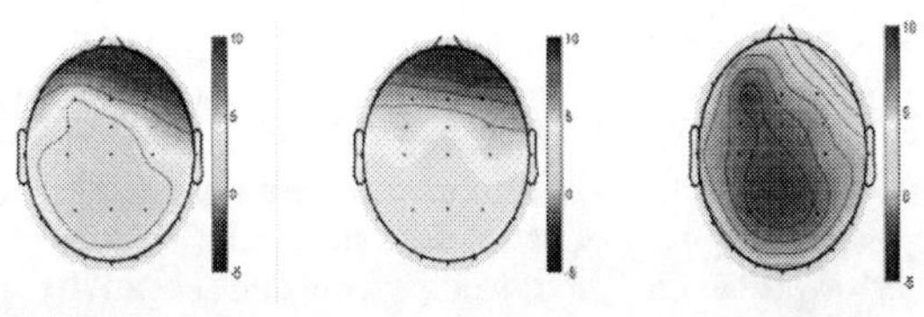

(a) (b) (c)

Figure 6. Head topography of the grand average waveforms for all participants considering an average window between $[200 \quad 300]$ ms after the feedback. (a) Raw Data ; (b) HAA Data and (c) Clean Data

A. Feedback-related negativity wave

According to the neuroscience literature, the feedback-related negativity (FRN) is an ERP component recorded in fronto-central areas of the scalp, which originates in the Anterior Cingulate Cortex (ACC) [17]. In this work, all regions were processed but only region $R3$ was chosen to be discussed, because the FRN effects were the strongest on it, in agreement with the existing literature. Figure 7 displays the grand-average waveforms of individual ERPs for the $R3$ region considering the two subsets of trials corresponding to the Right (ERPr) and Wrong (ERPw) answers, time-locked to the feedback. Thus, the value $0\ ms$ corresponds to the moment when the feedback occurred. In the displayed waveforms, we can observe large negative peaks after the feedback, peaking around $250\ ms$, which are consistent with the feedback-related negativity. As can be observed, the FRN wave in the wrong subset (dash line) is more prominent than in the right subset (solid line). Furthermore, an apparent difference between the Wrong and Right conditions is observed, with more negative amplitudes for the Wrong trials, Figure 7 (b),(c).

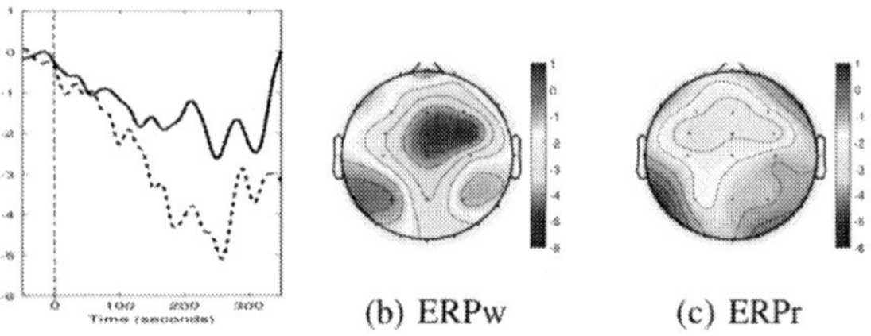

(a) FRN (b) ERPw (c) ERPr

Figure 7. FRN analysis: (a) Grand-average waveforms of individual ERPs in region $R3$ considering two subsets (ERPr and ERPw): Wrong response (dash line) and Right response (solid line). Head topography of the grand-average waveforms considering an average window between $[240\ \ 260]\ ms$ after the feedback: (b) Wrong subset and (c) Right subset

VII. Conclusion

The aim of the component selection method described in this paper is to remove high amplitude artifacts resulting from eye movements, patient movements, etc. It should be noted that this selection method is an alternative to those described in the literature as it is fully automatic and requires no input parameters to work. It is important to highlight the need to reduce the influence of high amplitude artifacts in EEG signals, not only to allow detection of ERP waves in neuroscience studies, but also for use of the EEG in BCI applications. Without doing so, one cannot be sure that the peaks observed in the signal reflect real brain processing and are not confounded with artifacts. After the preprocessing step, the data analysis revealed a frontocentral ERP wave related to error-processing: the feedback-related negativity (FRN), peaking around $250\ ms$, after feedback during performance on the HCT. As expected, errors elicited more negative amplitudes on that potential than correct responses.

Furthermore, results suggest that this error potential, FRN, might provide an adequate method for detecting errors that requires no additional processing time and could thereby improve the speed and accuracy of EEG-based communication with devices using BCI applications. The use of Error Potentials in BCI applications arises from the observation that this additional information provided automatically by the user could be used to improve the BCI performance.

Acknowledgment

This work was supported by FCT grant (Ref:SFRH/BPD/101112/2014)to Ana Rita Teixeira and Bial Foundation grant (Ref: 136/08) to Isabel Santos.

References

[1] M. Kirkove, C. François, and J. Verly, "Comparative evaluation of existing and new methods for correcting ocular artifacts in electroencephalographic recordings," Signal Processing, vol. 98, may 2014, pp. 102–120.

[2] A. K. Abdullah, C. Z. Zhang, A. A. A. Abdullah, and S. Lian, "Automatic Extraction System for Common Artifacts in EEG Signals Based on Evolutionary Stone's BSS Algorithm," Mathematical Problems in Engineering, vol. 2014, aug 2014, pp. 1–25.

[3] A. Delorme, T. Sejnowski, and S. Makeig, "Enhanced detection of artifacts in EEG data using higher-order statistics and independent component analysis." NeuroImage, vol. 34, no. 4, feb 2007, pp. 1443–9.

[4] L. Albera, A. Kachenoura, P. Comon, A. Karfoul, F. Wendling, L. Senhadji, and I. Merlet, "ICA-Based EEG denoising: a comparative analysis of fifteen methods," Bulletin of the Polish Academy of Sciences: Technical Sciences, vol. 60, no. 3, jan 2012, pp. 407–418.

[5] I. Daly, M. Billinger, R. Scherer, and G. Muller-Putz, "On the automated removal of artifacts related to head movement from the EEG." IEEE transactions on neural systems and rehabilitation engineering : a publication of the IEEE Engineering in Medicine and Biology Society, vol. 21, no. 3, may 2013, pp. 427–34.

[6] A. Mognon, J. Jovicich, L. Bruzzone, and M. Buiatti, "ADJUST: An automatic EEG artifact detector based on the joint use of spatial and temporal features." Psychophysiology, vol. 48, no. 2, feb 2011, pp. 229–40.

[7] H. Nolan, R. Whelan, and R. B. Reilly, "FASTER: Fully Automated Statistical Thresholding for EEG artifact Rejection." Journal of neuroscience methods, vol. 192, no. 1, sep 2010, pp. 152–62.

[8] W. Kong, Z. Zhou, S. Hu, J. Zhang, F. Babiloni, and G. Dai, "Automatic and direct identification of blink components from scalp EEG." Sensors (Basel, Switzerland), vol. 13, no. 8, jan 2013, pp. 10783–801.

[9] M. Silvetti, E. Nuñez Castellar, C. Roger, and T. Verguts, "Reward expectation and prediction error in human medial frontal cortex: an EEG study." NeuroImage, vol. 84, jan 2014, pp. 376–82.

[10] N. A. DeFilippis and E. McCampbell, The Booklet Category Test. Psychological Assessment Resources, 1997.

[11] M. Falkenstein, J. Hoormann, S. Christ, and J. Hohnsbein, "ERP components on reaction errors and their functional significance: A tutorial," Biological Psychology, vol. 51, no. 2-3, 2000, pp. 87–107.

[12] P. W. Ferrez and J. del R Millan, "Error-related EEG potentials generated during simulated brain-computer interaction." IEEE transactions on bio-medical engineering, vol. 55, no. 3, mar 2008, pp. 923–9.

[13] I. Iturrate, L. Montesano, and J. Minguez, "Task-dependent signal variations in EEG error-related potentials for braincomputer interfaces," Journal of Neural Engineering, vol. 10, no. 2, apr 2013, p. 026024.

[14] I. Daly, N. Nicolaou, S. J. Nasuto, and K. Warwick, "Automated artifact removal from the electroencephalogram: a comparative study." Clinical EEG and neuroscience, vol. 44, no. 4, oct 2013, pp. 291–306.

[15] A. Tome and E. Lang, "Approximate diagonalization approach to blind source separation with a subset of matrices," in Seventh International Symposium on Signal Processing and Its Applications, 2003. Proceedings., vol. 2. IEEE, 2003, pp. 105–108 vol.2.

[16] A. Cichocki and S.-i. Amari, Adaptive Blind Signal and Image Processing: Learning Algorithms and Applications, Volume 1, 2002.

[17] W. H. R. Miltner, C. H. Braun, and M. G. H. Coles, "Event-related brain potentials following incorrect feedback in a time-estimation task: Evidence for a generic neural system for error detection," J. Cognitive Neuroscience, vol. 9, no. 6, 1997, pp. 788–798.

Analysis of Emotions in Vowels: a Recurrence Approach

Angela Lombardi, Pietro Guccione

Dipartimento di Ingegneria Elettrica e dell'Informazione
Politecnico di Bari
Email: angela.lombardi@poliba.it, pietro.guccione@poliba.it

Abstract—**Emotional content in speech has been so far characterized by features based on linear source-filter models. However, the presence of nonlinear and chaotic phenomena in speech generation have been widely proven in literature. In this work, a novel framework has been developed to explore recurrence properties of vowels and describe nonlinear dynamics of speech. Experiments using a database of short spoken sentences emitted in the six basic emotions (anger, boredom, fear, happiness, neutral, sadness) show preliminary results of the approach.**

Keywords–Speech Emotion Recognition; Recurrence Plot; Recurrence Quantitative Analysis.

I. INTRODUCTION

Speech Emotion Recognition (SER) is a recent field of research that aims at identifying the emotional state of a speaker through a collection of machine learning and pattern recognition techniques [1].

As a classification problem, a SER system needs a set of features able to optimally reflect the emotional content in speech. According to the existing literature, it is possible to distinguish three main categories of features: prosodic, spectral, and quality-based [2]. Prosodic features such as the fundamental frequency (pitch), the energy of the signal and the rhythm/articulation rate, have been combined with spectral measures (Mel Frequency Cepstral Coefficients (MFCC), Linear Predictor Cepstral Coefficients (LPCC) and formants) in different ways to improve the performances of the classifier [3]. The third category includes acoustic cues related to the shape of glottal pulse signal, its amplitude variation (shimmer) and frequency variation (jitter) [4].

Although such features have been extensively used for the development of SER systems, they are based on a source-filter model [5], which represents a simplification of the process of voice production that ignores more complex physiological mechanisms. In fact, in the last two decades, nonlinear tools for speech signal processing have spread out after new findings concerning the occurrence of nonlinear phenomena during voice production [6]. In particular, the evidence of the chaotic behavior of certain processes involved in the speech generation (e.g., turbulent airflow) [7], made the *Chaos Theory* a favored approach for the study of nonlinear dynamics in the system voice.

To describe these dynamics it is necessary to find the set of the possible states that the system can take (to reconstruct the phase space). This approach assumes that the speech signal represents a projection of a higher-dimensional nonlinear dynamical system evolving in time, with unknown characteristics. Embedding techniques can be employed to reconstruct the attractor of the system in the phase space and provide a representation of its trajectories. Afterward, it is possible to describe the dynamic behavior of the system by studying the properties of the embedded attractor: chaotic measures such as Lyapunov exponents, correlation dimension and entropy, have been successfully applied to the analysis of vocal pathologies and speech nonlinearities [8] [9].

The behavior of the trajectories of a system in the phase space can also be modeled through the recurrence, a property that quantifies the tendency of a system to return to a state close to the initial one. A Recurrence Plot (RP) is a graphic tool that shows the recurrent behavior of the trajectories of a system even with high-dimensional phase space [10]. Recurrence Quantitative Analysis (RQA) has been introduced later to objectively evaluate the structures contained in a RP through nonlinear measurements. RQA has found extensive applications in many scientific fields, thanks to its effectiveness in the presence of short and non-stationary data [11] [12].

In this work, we have developed a framework to explore the recurrence properties of vowel segments taken from a set of spoken sentences of a publicly available database, for six categories of basic emotions (anger, boredom, fear, happiness, neutral, sadness). An automatic vowel extraction module has been built up to extract vowel segments from each sentence; then, their time evolutions have been analyzed by means of the RQA measures. To test the ability of these measures to characterize the different emotional contents, they have been grouped according to the emotion which they belong to and statistical tests have been performed to compare the six groups.

The rest of the paper is divided in four sections: the theoretical background is provided in Section II, the general framework of the approach is explained in Section III, results and conclusions are reported in Section IV and Section V, respectively.

II. THEORETICAL BACKGROUND

This section provides a general overview of the basic concepts related to the state space reconstruction of a dynamical system and of the main tools used for the analysis of its recurrence properties.

A. The Embedding Theorem

The state of a dynamical system is determined by the values of the variables that describe it at a given time.

However, in a real scenario, not all the variables of the system can be inferred and often only a time series $\{u_i\}_{i=1}^{N}$ is available as an output of the system.

Takens demonstrated that it is possible to use time delayed versions of the signal at the output of the system to reconstruct a phase space topologically equivalent to the original one. According to Takens' embedding theorem [13], a state in the reconstructed phase space is given by a m-dimensional time delay embedded vector:

$$\vec{x}_i = \left(u_i, u_{i+\tau}, \ldots, u_{i+(m-1)\tau}\right) \quad (1)$$

where m is the embedding dimension and τ is the time delay. For the embedded parameters estimation, several techniques have been proposed. As an example, the First Local Minimum of Average Mutual Information algorithm [14] can be used to determine the time delay, while the False Nearest-Neighbors algorithm [15] is usually employed to estimate the minimum embedding dimension.

B. Recurrence Plots

A Recurrence Plot is a graphical tool that provides a representation of recurrent states of a dynamical system through a square matrix:

$$R_{i,j}(\epsilon) = \Theta\left(\epsilon - \|\vec{x_i} - \vec{x_j}\|\right), \quad i,j = 1,...,N \quad (2)$$

with $\vec{x_i}, \vec{x_j}$ the system state at times i, j, Θ the Heaviside function, ϵ a threshold for closeness, N the number of considered states and $\|\cdot\|$ a norm function.

An entry of the matrix is set equal to one if the distance between the corresponding pair of neighboring states is below the threshold ϵ and zero elsewhere.

The resulting plot is symmetric and always exhibits the main diagonal, called line of identity (LOI). Apart for the general RP structure, it is often possible to distinguish small scale structures, which show local (temporal) relationships of the segments of the system trajectory (for a visual reference, see Figure 3). In details:

- single isolated points are related to rare states;
- diagonal lines parallel to the LOI indicate that the evolution of states is similar at different times;
- vertical lines mark time intervals in which states do not change.

C. Recurrence Quantitative Analysis

Several measures of complexity (RQA) have been proposed to obtain an objective quantification of the patterns in a Recurrence Plot [11] [12].

RQA can be divided into three major classes:

1) Measures based on recurrence density. Among these, the simplest measure is the *recurrence rate* (RR) defined as:

$$RR(\epsilon) = \frac{1}{N^2}\sum_{i,j=1}^{N} R_{i,j}(\epsilon) \quad (3)$$

It is a measure of the density of the recurrence points in the RP.

2) Measures based on the distribution $P(l)$ of lengths l of the diagonal lines. Among these, the *determinism* (DET) is the ratio of the recurrence points that form diagonal structures to all recurrence points and it is an index of the predictability of a system:

$$DET = \frac{\sum_{l=l_{min}}^{N} lP(l)}{\sum_{l=1}^{N} lP(l)} \quad (4)$$

The $RATIO$, defined as the ratio between DET and RR, combines the advantages of the these two categories of measures: it has been proven that it is able to detect some types of transitions in particular dynamics.

3) Measures based on the distribution $P(v)$ of vertical line lengths v. This distribution is used to quantify laminar phases during which the states of a system change very slowly or do not change at all. The ratio of recurrence points forming vertical structures to all recurrence points of the RP is called *laminarity* (LAM):

$$LAM = \frac{\sum_{v=v_{min}}^{N} vP(v)}{\sum_{l=1}^{N} vP(v)} \quad (5)$$

From a Recurrence Plot, it is possible to extrapolate the *recurrence times*. The *recurrence times of second type* are:

$$\left\{T_k^{(2)} = j'_{k+1} - j'_k\right\}_{k\in\mathbb{N}} \quad (6)$$

The set of $T^{(2)}$ measure the time distance between the beginning of subsequent recurrence structures in the RP along the vertical direction and they can be considered as an estimate of the average of the lengths of white vertical lines in a column of the plot [12].

A great advantage offered by this analysis is that the calculation of the RQA measures for moving windows along the RP allows to identify the transitions of dynamical systems.

III. GENERAL FRAMEWORK

The algorithm block scheme is represented in Figure 1. Since the voice has a non-stationary nature, we perform a short term analysis with a frame size of 40 ms and an overlap of 50%. Given an input track, an automatic vowel extraction module is used to detect and retain only the vowel frames and for each of them the optimal parameters (m and τ) for state space reconstruction are found. Then, RPs are generated using the time delay method, and some RQA measures extracted to describe RPs quantitatively. Since a set of RQA measures can be extracted, in principle, for each frame, statistics on these measures may be collected to give a general description of the emotional content of the input sentence.

Each step of the adopted framework is detailed in the following sections.

A. Database

The German Berlin Emotional Speech Database (EmoDB) [16] has been employed for all the experiments carried out in this work. The database contains ten sentences pronounced by ten actors (five males and five females) in 7 different emotional states: neutral, anger, fear, happiness, sadness, disgust and boredom. The audio tracks were sampled as mono signals at 16 KHz, with 8 bit/sample. Most of the sentences were recorded several times in different versions and the resulting corpus was subjected to a perception test where the degree of recognition of emotions and their naturalness were evaluated by a group of listeners. Utterances with an emotion recognition rate better than 80% and a naturalness score greater than 60% were included in the final database. As shown in Table I, among the 535 available sentences, some emotions prevail over

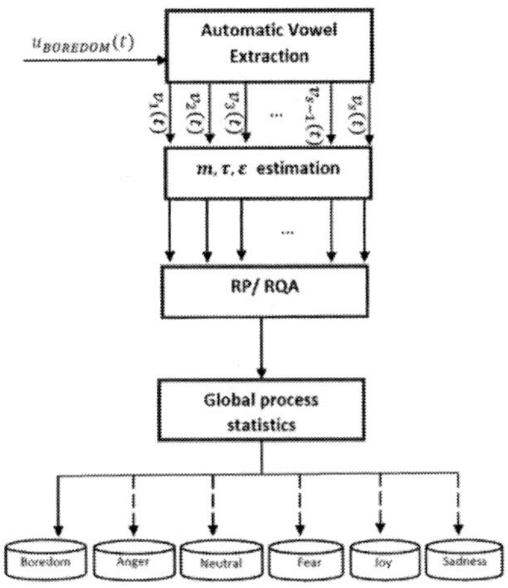

Figure 1. The algorithm block scheme for an example input sentence.

the others. The emotion disgust has been excluded from our analysis because of the too low number of tracks belonging to this group.

TABLE I. NUMBER OF UTTERANCES IN EMODB

Emotion	# of utterances
Anger	127
Boredom	81
Disgust	46
Fear	69
Happiness	71
Neutral	79
Sadness	62

B. *Automatic Vowel Extraction*

The vocal tract acts as a resonator filter which has its own resonance frequencies known as formants: by varying the shape of the vocal tract to produce different sounds, the formant frequencies of the filter change too [5]. Therefore, lots of characteristics of speech sounds can be detected by analyzing the spectral content of their waveforms. In detail, vowels, unlike consonants, show quasi-periodic waveforms and this can be proved by differences in the first three formant frequencies [5].

For these reasons, the estimation of the vowel segments has been carried on by extracting spectral features from the formant frequencies estimated from the power spectral density of the audio track. Then, the features have been used to train a classifier that automatically detects vowel segments in the signal.

Supposing each frame the output of a stationary process, an autoregressive model (AR) has been used to estimate the power spectral density. First, the order of the model has been identified with the Akaike's Information Criterion (AIC) [17] to avoid splitting line and spurious peaks in the final spectrum. Subsequently, the Burg's method [18] has been employed to find the parameters of the AR model. This technique has been preferred over the simple linear prediction analysis as the former identifies the optimal set of parameters by minimizing the sums of squares of the forward and backward prediction errors while the latter uses only the backward errors. Furthermore, as compared with other parametric methods, the Burg's algorithm ensures more stable models and a higher frequency resolution [19].

The peaks of the power spectral density are in correspondence of the formants position. The first three peaks have been identified in the estimated spectrum and for each of them the following characteristics have been collected:

- the frequency at which they occur;
- the amplitude of the peak;
- the area under the spectral envelope within the -3dB bandwidth.

To distinguish the vowel sounds from all other types of phonemes (including silence intervals) a one-class classification approach has been adopted. This method was introduced by Schölkopf [20] as a variant of the two-class SVM to identify a set of outliers amongst examples of the single class under consideration. Thus, according to this approach, the outlier data are examples of the negative class (in this case, the not-vowels frames). A kernel function is used to map the data into a feature space F in which the origin is the representative point of the negative class. So, the SVM returns a function f that assigns the value $+1$ in a subspace in which the most of the data points are located and the opposite value -1 elsewhere, in order to separate the examples of the class of interest from the origin of the feature space with the maximum margin.

Formally, let us consider $\mathbf{x}_1, \mathbf{x}_2, \ldots, \mathbf{x}_l$, l training vectors of the one class X, where X is a compact subset of $\mathbb{R}^N$. Let $\Phi : X \rightarrow F$ be a a kernel function that map the training vectors into another space F. Separating the data set from the origin is equivalent to solving the following quadratic problem:

$$\min_{w \in F, \xi \in \mathbb{R}^l, \rho \in \mathbb{R}} \frac{1}{2}||w||^2 \frac{1}{\nu l} \sum_{i=1}^{l} \xi_i - \rho \tag{7}$$

subject to

$$(w \cdot \Phi(\mathbf{x}_i)) \geq \rho - \xi_i, \quad \xi_i \geq 0 \tag{8}$$

where $\nu \in (0; 1]$ is a parameter that controls the decision boundary of the classification problem, ξ_i are the nonzero slack variables, w a weight vector and ρ an offset that parametrizes a hyperplane in the feature space associated with the kernel. If w and ρ solve for this problem, then the decision function:

$$f(\mathbf{x}) = \mathrm{sign}(w \cdot \Phi(\mathbf{x}) - \rho) \tag{9}$$

will be positive for the most of the examples $\mathbf{x}_i$ contained in the training set.

Of course, the type of kernel function, the operating parameters of the kernel and the correct value of ν must be estimated to build the one-class SVM classifier. As suggested by the author, we have chosen a Gaussian kernel with Sequential Minimal Optimization (SMO) algorithm to train the classifier, since the data are always separable from the origin in the feature space. For generic patterns $\mathbf{x}$ and $\mathbf{y}$, a Gaussian kernel is expressed as:

$$k(\mathbf{x}, \mathbf{y}) = \exp(\frac{||\mathbf{x} - \mathbf{y}||^2}{c}) \tag{10}$$

where the parameter c is the kernel scale that controls the tradeoff between the over-fitting and under-fitting loss in the feature space F.

Regarding the choice of the value ν, it should be taken into account that it represents an upper bound on the fraction of outliers and, at the same time, a lower bound on the fraction of support vectors. It is then necessary to find a value that on the one hand is able to to describe the whole dataset for training and on the other hand avoids the over-training of such data. Results on the tuning of the parameters on real data and classification performances are in Section IV-A.

C. RP/RQA

In this work, the dynamics of each vowel were treated as local descriptions of the overall process of expression of a particular emotion. Therefore, after extraction of vowel segments from a sentence, a frame-level analysis is applied to monitor such dynamics. First, time delays and embedding dimensions are estimated to allow a correct reconstruction of the dynamics in the phase space. Hence the Recurrence Plots are obtained and the Recurrence Quantitative Analysis is performed on RPs. In order to explore the time dependent behavior of the recurrence measures, the computation is performed using sliding windows of length W (less than the duration of a frame) with an offset of W_s samples along the main diagonal of the RP of each vowel frame. The values of these two parameters are calculated accounting for the scale of the dynamics to be investigated (local/global) and for the temporal resolution to be achieved. The overall trend of each RQA measure is finally reconstructed considering the various vowel segments neatly placed in the sentence. For an experimental dataset of sentences, the trends of each RQA measures are grouped by emotion and some statistics are computed to explore the general characteristics of the emotions expressed in the sentences.

IV. RESULTS

The following sections report the performances achieved by the one-class SVM classifier and both qualitative and quantitative results of the recurrence analysis.

A. Automatic Vowel Extraction

To train the one class SVM classifier, a dataset was used of 128 segments of German vowels of duration equal to 40 ms, extracted from several sentences spoken by four people (two men and two women) for the six emotions. In order to identify the optimal values for the parameters c and ν, the classifier was trained and validated several times. In particular, due to the nature of the classification problem, an holdout validation scheme has been adopted. So, another set of 83 speech segments including vowels, consonants and pauses, has been used to tune the parameters and identify the most effective model. Keeping fixed the value of ν, the classifier was retrained by varying the value of the kernel scale in a predetermined range. For each model obtained, the performances on the validation set were evaluated in terms of accuracy, sensitivity (or true positive rate), specificity (or true negative rate) and false positive rate. The curves that illustrate the behavior of such measures for three values of ν and by varying the kernel scale from 0 to 2.7 are shown in Figure 2.

In Figure 2b and 2c only one point can be identified to guarantee high performances of the classifier, since the values of accuracy, sensitivity and specificity are high (around 0.7), while the false positive rate remains low. For kernel scale

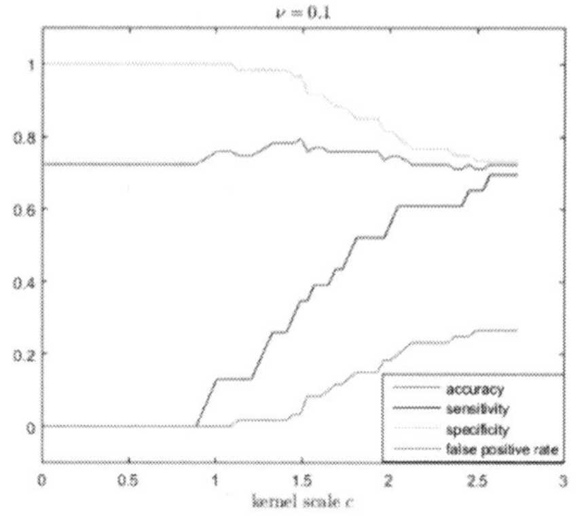

(a)

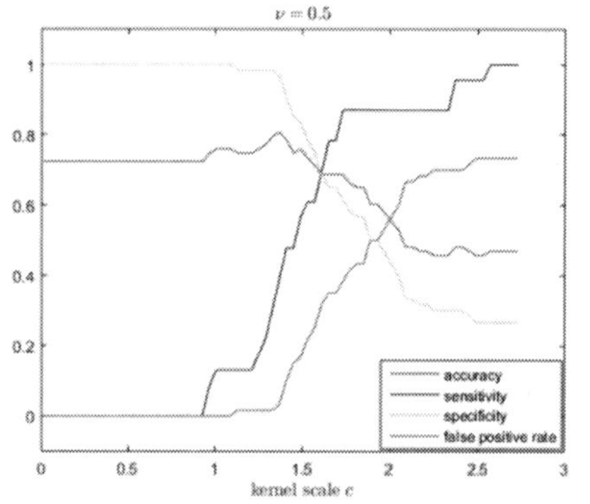

(b)

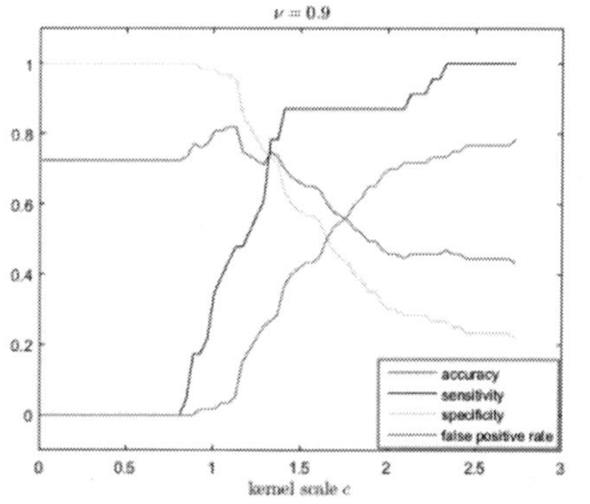

(c)

Figure 2. Accuracy, sensitivity, specificity and false positive rate of the one class SVM classifier in function of the kernel scale c for the fixed parameter (a) $\nu = 0.1$ (b) $\nu = 0.5$ (c) $\nu = 0.9$.

values greater than this optimum, specificity and accuracy decrease rapidly, while sensitivity and false positive rate increase. These results suggest that there is a rapid growth of the number of false positives, i.e., the percentage of the not-vowels frames incorrectly predicted as vowels by the classifier increases.

For our purposes, the system critically depends on the percentage of false positives, since the classifier acts properly if it is capable of rejecting the greatest amount of not-vowel frames. Therefore, even at the expense of a lower number of true positives and higher percentage of false negatives

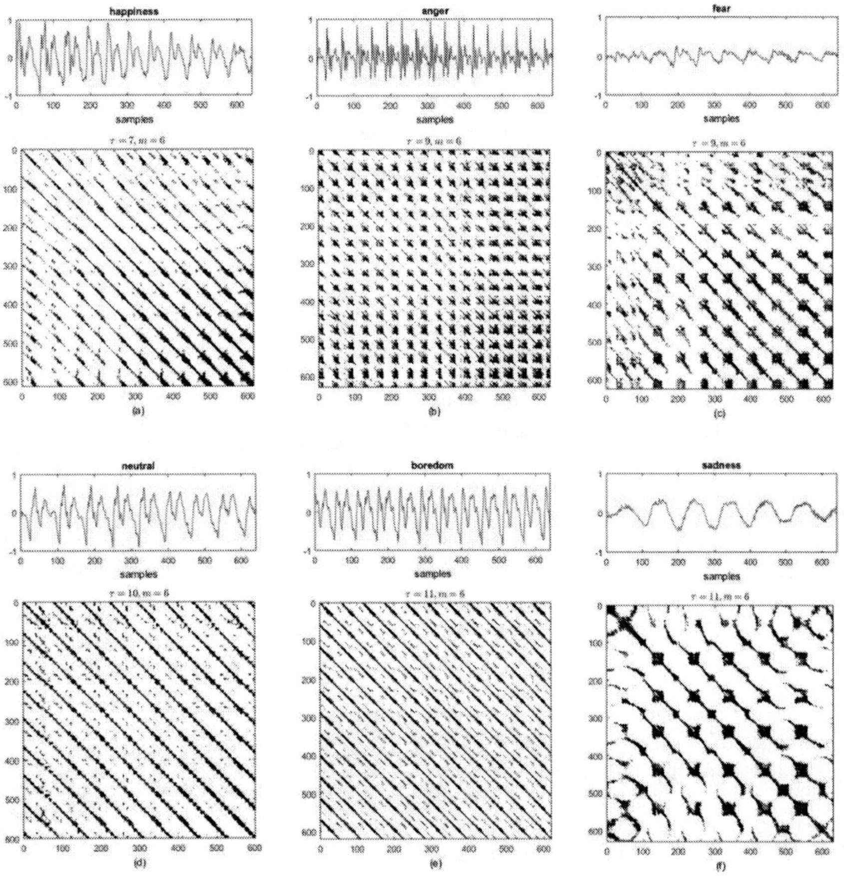

Figure 3. RPs of vowel /a/ in the track $08a02$ for emotions: (a) happiness, (b) anger, (c) fear, (d) neutral, (e) boredom, (f) sadness; ϵ is setting to 10% of maximum space diameter with a maximum norm.

(vowel frames incorrectly rejected), we have preferred to set $\nu = 0.1$ and consequently chosen the value of c at which the classifier returns high values of accuracy and specificity, while maintaining a false positive rate less than 15% (see Figure 2a).

To assess the performances of the one class SVM with the chosen parameter settings ($\nu = 0.1$ and $c = 1.75$), we performed a final test on a set of 40 speech segments independent of both the training and the validation sets. The confusion matrix is shown in Table II. As it can be seen, the low rate of false positives (not-vowels incorrectly predicted as vowel frames) confirms the validity of the model for the selected parameters (represented in Figure 2a for $\nu = 0.1$ and $c = 1.75$).

TABLE II. CONFUSION MATRIX OF THE ONE CLASS SVM ON THE TEST SET COMPOSED OF 20 VOWEL AND 20 NOT-VOWEL FRAMES.

		Predicted condition	
		Vowels	Not-vowels
True conditions	Vowels	9	11
	Not-vowels	4	16

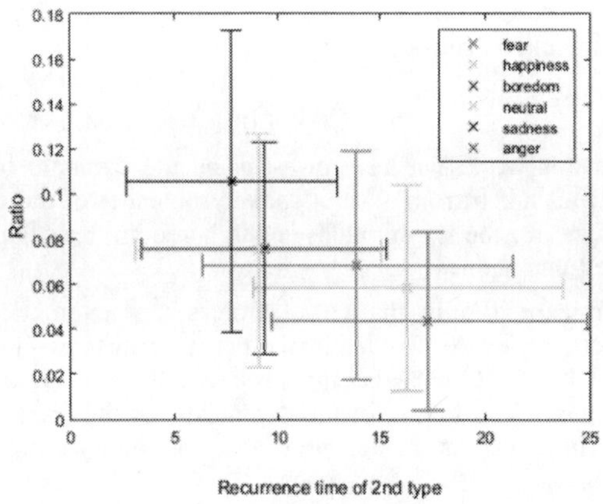

Figure 4. Median and iqr values of $RATIO$ and $T^{(2)}$ measures for the six groups of emotions.

B. Qualitative and quantitative results: RP-RQA

The patterns in RPs can reveal typical behaviors of the system and so they can be used to provide a general description of the time evolution of the dynamic trajectories. Figure 3 shows the RPs of the vowel /a/ extracted in the same sentence and approximately in the same position, pronounced by a female subject for different emotions. As it can be seen, all RPs have a topology with periodic patterns that are regularly repeated, with the exception of the emotion fear in which there are discontinuities and white bands that indicate the presence of abrupt changes in the dynamics of the system. Another distinctive feature is the length of the diagonal lines: the RPs of boredom and neutral, besides being very similar each other, have the longest diagonal lines; on the other hand, anger and fear show very short diagonal lines. Moreover, a drift can be noted in the emotion sadness: the RP fades away from LOI indicating that the system varies very slowly. The examples show that certain measures are most distinctive for some emotions and that certainly the density of points in the RPs, the length of the lines present in them and measures that are able to differentiate the different kinds of time periodicity (such as $T^{(2)}$), can effectively distinguish among different emotional levels.

On the basis of such considerations we performed the analysis described in Section III-C on a set of tracks in EmoDB (obtained by excluding from the entire set of tracks in the database, those used to train the one class SVM), to extract the collection of $RATIO$ and $T^{(2)}$ values along time. The measures were then grouped by emotions for the same RQA, obtaining 2 sets of measures (each set consists of 6 groups of data, one for each emotion). The non-parametric Kruskal-Wallis test was employed for testing whether the 6 different data groups of each RQA measure originate from the same distribution (null hypothesis), at a significance level $\alpha = 0.05$. Both tests returned a p-value < 0.0001, so the null hypothesis was rejected.

In order to better appreciate the possible differences among populations, median and interquartile range (iqr) values of the 2 RQA measures for all the groups of emotions were computed and are reported in Figure 4. It is noteworthy that boredom and neutral exhibit very similar values and that there is a relationship between the position of the emotion (based on the median values) on the 2D plot and their levels of activation (the so called arousal).

V. CONCLUSIONS

In this work, we have investigated the dynamic behavior of vowels taken from a set of spoken sentences of the EmoDB database, for the six emotions anger, boredom, fear, happiness, neutral and sadness.

To extract only the vowel frames, an automatic vowel extraction module was implemented. It consists essentially in a one class SVM classifier that processes the not-vowels frame as outliers. The tuning of the parameters of the classifier and an accurate validation step allowed us to identify a model able to achieve the 79% of accuracy.

Supposing that the expression of a particular emotional content in a spoken sentence is a gradual complex process, we exploited some properties of the local dynamics of the vowels in it to understand certain aspects of the overall process. The behavior of the trajectories of vowels dynamics was explored by means of RPs. Two kinds of RQA measures were extracted to describe RPs quantitatively. Statistical tests confirm that the considered RQA measures result statistically significant for discriminating the six groups of emotions.

In conclusion, it can be observed that certain RQA measures can better discriminate among the basic emotions examined. However, a further development could include a multivariate analysis to identify a specific subset of measures that perform a better and more complete characterization of the different emotional levels.

REFERENCES

[1] C. N. Anagnostopoulos, T. Iliou, and I. Giannoukos, "Features and classifiers for emotion recognition from speech: a survey from 2000 to 2011," Artificial Intelligence Review, vol.43(2), 2015, pp. 155-177.

[2] M. E. Ayadi, M .S. Kamel, and F. Karray, "Survey on speech emotion recognition: Features, classification schemes, and databases," Pattern Recognition, vol. 44(3), 2011, pp. 572-587.

[3] I. Luengo, E. Navas, and I. Hernáez, "Feature Analysis and Evaluation for Automatic Emotion Identification in Speech," IEEE Trans. Multimedia, vol. 12(6), 2010, pp. 490-501.

[4] M. Lugger and B. Yang, "The relevance of voice quality features in speaker independent emotion recognition," in Proc. Int. Conf. Acoustics, Speech and Signal Processing, Honolulu, HI, vol. 4, Apr. 2007, pp. 17-20.

[5] G. Fant, Acoustic Theory of Speech Production, Mouton & Co., the Hague, 1960.

[6] I. R. Titze, R. Baken, and H. Herzel, "Evidence of chaos in vocal fold vibration," New Frontiers in Basic Science, I.R. Titze. Ed. Vocal Fold Physiology, San Diego, CA: Singular Publishing Group, 1993, pp. 143-188.

[7] H. Herzel, "Bifurcations and Chaos in Voice Signals," Applied Mechanics Reviews, vol. 46(7), 1993, pp. 399-413.

[8] P. Henriquez, et al., "Characterization of Healthy and Pathological Voice Through Measures Based on Nonlinear Dynamics," IEEE Transactions on Audio, Speech, and Language Processing, vol. 17(6), 2009, pp. 1186-1195.

[9] J. D. Arias-Londoño, J. I. Godino-Llorente, N. Sáenz-Lechón, V. Osma-Ruiz, and G. Castellanos-Domínguez, "Automatic Detection of Pathological Voices Using Complexity Measures, Noise Parameters, and Mel-Cepstral Coefficients," IEEE Transactions on Biomedical Engineering, vol. 58(2), 2011, pp. 370-379.

[10] J. P. Eckmann, S. O. Kamphorst, and D. Ruelle, "Recurrence plots of dynamical systems," Europhys. Lett. vol. 5, 1987, pp. 973-977.

[11] J. P. Zbilut and C. L. Webber Jr., "Embeddings and delays as derived from quantification of recurrence plots," Phys. Lett. A vol. 171(3-4), 1992, pp. 199-203.

[12] N. Marwan, M. C. Romano, M. Thiel, and J. Kurths, "Recurrence Plots for the Analysis of Complex Systems," Physics Reports vol. 438(5-6), 2007, pp. 237-329.

[13] F. Takens, "Detecting strange attractors in turbulence," Lectures Notes in Mathematics, Vol. 898, 1981, pp. 366-381, Springer.

[14] A. M. Fraser and H. L. Swinney, "Independent coordinates for strange attractors from mutual information," Phys. Rev. A, vol. 33, 1986, pp. 1134-1140.

[15] M. B. Kennel, R. Brown, and H. D. I. Abarbanel, "Determining embedding dimension for phase-space reconstruction using a geometrical construction," Phys. Rev. A, vol. 45, 1992, pp. 3403-3411.

[16] F. Burkhardt, A. Paeschke, M. Rolfes, W. Sendlmeier, and B. Weiss, "A database of german emotional speech," Proceedings on Interspeech, Lisbon, Portugal, 2005, pp. 1517-1520.

[17] H. Akaike, "A new look at the statistical model identification," IEEE Transaction on Automatic Control, vol. 19(6), 1974, pp. 716-723.

[18] J. P. Burg, "Maximum entropy spectral analysis," in Proc. 37th Meet. Soc. Explorational Geophys., Oklahoma City, 1967.

[19] B. I. Helme and Ch. L. Nikias, "Improved spectrum performance via a data-adaptive weighted Burg technique," IEEE Transactions on Acoustics, Speech, and Signal Processing, vol. 33(4), 1985, pp. 903-910.

[20] B. Schölkopf, J. C. Platt, J. Shawe-Taylor, A. J. Smola, and R. C. Williamson, "Estimating the support of a high-dimensional distribution," Technical report, Microsoft Research, MSR-TR-99-87, 1999.

Efficient Clustering and on-board ROI-based Compression for Hyperspectral Radar

Rossella Giordano, Angela Lombardi, Pietro Guccione

Dipartimento di Ingegneria Elettrica e dell'Informazione
Politecnico di Bari
Email: giordanorossella88@gmail.com, angela.lombardi@poliba.it, pietro.guccione@poliba.it

Abstract—**In recent years, hyperspectral sensors for remote sensing of the Earth have become very popular. Such systems are able to provide the user with images having both spectral and spatial information. The current hyperspectral spaceborne sensors are able to capture large areas with increased spatial and spectral resolution. For this reason, the volume of acquired data must be reduced on-board in order to avoid a low orbital duty cycle due to limited storage space. Recently, literature have focused the attention to efficient way of on-board data compression, since this is a challenge task due to the difficult environment (outer space), and due to the limited power and computing resources. The current work proposes a framework for on-board operations such as: automatic recognition of target types or detection of events in near real time, in regions of interest with an unsupervised classifier; the compression of specific regions with different bit rates compared to the remaining acquisition (background); the management of the data volume to be transmitted to the Ground Station. Experiments are shown using real data taken from AVIRIS airborne sensor in a harbor area.**

Keywords–Hyperspectral; ROI; clustering; on-board compression.

I. Introduction

A hyperspectral dataset is a data cube composed by a number of images equal to the number of bands in which the sensor has acquired and size equal to that of the captured area. Hyperspectral images are used in a wide variety of applications like: analysis of type of vegetation, monitoring of the forest condition (biomass, deforestation, changes with seasonal cycles), monitoring of coastline and glaciers (glaciers erosion), monitoring of the environment disasters (forest fires, oil spill, flooding) and so on [1].

The high dimensionality of hyperspectral data is very advantageous for the image analysis but, at the same time, the on-board storage space and the transmission bandwidth are limited resources. For this reason, it is necessary to set a proper system of on-board data compression before the transmission to the Ground Station.

Usually, hyperspectral images show high spatial correlation among neighbor pixels and correlation among bands. Such properties have been exploited by compression algorithms to remove the redundance. There are many ways of analysis for redundancy reduction described in literature: these are divided into transformed-based and predictors-based. The transformed-based methods use Discrete Wavelet Transform (DWT) or Discrete Cosine Transform (DCT) [2]. The wavelet transform method offers an efficient rate-distortion and for this reason it has been implemented within the JPEG2000 standard, which is currently the most advanced and efficient compression way for images [3].

The proposed framework aims: (i) at recognizing specific regions of interest (ROIs) using a someway commanded query (generated by the on-ground user) and by means of a computationally efficient clustering algorithm and (ii) to make a differential efficient compression of the regions on the basis of a hierarchy specified in the query (region of interest, medium interest, background). Comparison of the algorithm efficiency is carried on with current JPEG2000 standard in terms of generated data volume and distortion level on the regions of interest.

The rest of the paper is organized as follows: the adopted framework is presented in Section II, the results of the experiments are shown in Section III, and finally the conclusions are reported in Section IV.

II. General Framework

The work has been carried out in two steps.

During the first step, it is supposed that the system is able to recognize specific regions of interest (particular topographic classes, specific events as disaster or limited areas), according to external commands or specific query. Starting from this nontrivial hypothesis, a clustering algorithm is applied to the acquired image to isolate the class or region of interest. The clustering resorts to methods already known in literature (to simplify the on-board process) such as the k-means clustering, but an automatic estimation of some critical parameters is applied for a quicker and more efficient on-board implementation.

The second step consists in the encoding and compression of the ROIs identified in the first step. The aim of these operations is to encode the ROIs with a higher bit rate since they represent the areas of interest for the user, while the remaining part of the image (that we shall call the background) using a lower bit rate.

The overall algorithm has, this way, certainly a distortion rate that is lower than that of a comparing standard as JPEG2000. However, over the specific area of interest, the distortion can be reduced even using the same average bit rate. An alternative comparison with JPEG2000 accounts for the same distortion and compares the data volume generate in the two cases.

The diagram of the implemented algorithm is shown in Figure1.

A. Clustering algorithm for detection

Unsupervised classification methods are more suitable for automatic segmentation and identification of ROIs in hyperspectral images. Clustering algorithms, starting from a data

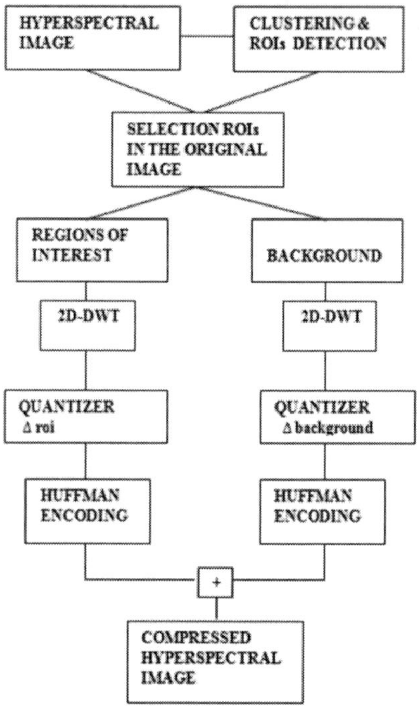

Figure 1. Block diagram of the implemented algorithm.

set, are able to identify significant patterns without knowning labels and, consequently, they do not need of training phases to improve the performances of an automatic classifier. For these reasons, clustering methods can bring significant benefits:

- it is not necessary to employ considerable resources to learn features of a large set of images to identify ROIs, making the application general purpose;
- by using the intrinsic characteristics of the image, the computational time is reduced, making possible a real time (or near-real time) automatic detection of ROIs;
- the characteristics of some patterns may change over time, but a clustering algorithm can easily follow such variations.

One of the most efficient clustering algorithm known in literature is the K-means [4]: through an iterative procedure, K partitions of the points in the initial set are identified by minimizing the sum of squares of distances between the centroid of each partition and all the other points of the set. A great advantage offered by this process is the high convergence speed, while the identification of the optimal parameter K represents a critical step.

In this work, the pixel spectral depth has been employed to make an unsupervised classification of the regions by means of the K-means algorithm. An automated method that exploits the statistical characteristics of the image [5] has been improved to fix the number of clusters K: from the three-dimensional co-occurrence matrices of the hyperspectral cube [6], information about the patterns of pixels of the entire 3D structure have been extracted to calculate the optimal value of K.

For a two-dimensional image quantized to n levels of gray, a co-occurrence matrix (GLCM) describes the spatial relationship among gray level values and it consists of a $n \times n$ array obtained by specifying the separation distance between two pixels (i.e., the offset) and the direction along which to cross the image. These two sets of information can be synthesized through a displacement vector $d = (dx, dy)$, where dx represents the offset in the x direction and dy is the offset value in the y direction of the input image. Each entry (i, j) in the matrix represents the total number of times that the pixel with value i occurred in the specified spatial relationship to a pixel with value j in the input image, hence the matrix provides information about the different combinations of pixel gray levels existing in an image.

Formally, for an image I of size $P \times Q$, the gray-level co-occurrence matrix C is defined as:

$$C(i,j) = \sum_{i=1}^{P} \sum_{j=1}^{Q} \begin{cases} 1, & \text{if } I(x,y) = i \wedge I(x+dx, y+dy) = j \\ 0, & \text{otherwise} \end{cases} \tag{1}$$

In hyperspectral images, it may not be appropriate to analyze independently the individual spectral bands. To extract both spatial and spectral information, co-occurrence matrices for volumetric data (3D GLCM) have been adopted. These matrices are able to capture the spatial dependence of gray-level values across spectral bands. A 3D GLCM is defined by specifying a displacement vector $d = (dx, dy, dz)$, where dx and dy are the same as described for 2D matrices, and dz represents the offset distance along the spectral axis of the hyperspectral image. However, while for a 2D GLCM only 4 displacement directions are possible, in the three-dimensional case, there are 26 admissible co-occurrence directions and only 13 of them differ from each other. The 13 directions and their corresponding displacement vectors are reported in Table I, where D is the offset distance between the pixel of interest and its neighbors, θ is measured in the XY plane in the positive x direction, and ϕ is the angle between the vector which identifies the pixel along the spectral direction and the XY plane. A graphical presentation of the pixel of interest X_0 and the 13 adjacent pixels X_i, $i = 1, \ldots, 13$ in the directions specified in Table I is shown in Figure 2.

TABLE I. DISPLACEMENT VECTORS AND DIRECTIONS OF CO-OCCURRENCE MATRICES FOR VOLUMETRIC DATA.

Displacement vectors	Directions (θ, ϕ)
$(D, 0, D)$	$(0^\circ, 45^\circ)$
$(D, 0, 0)$	$(0^\circ, 90^\circ)$
$(D, 0, -D)$	$(0^\circ, 135^\circ)$
(D, D, D)	$(45^\circ, 45^\circ)$
$(D, D, 0)$	$(45^\circ, 90^\circ)$
$(D, D, -D)$	$(45^\circ, 135^\circ)$
$(0, D, D)$	$(90^\circ, 45^\circ)$
$(0, D, 0)$	$(90^\circ, 90^\circ)$
$(0, D, -D)$	$(90^\circ, 135^\circ)$
$(-D, D, D)$	$(135^\circ, 45^\circ)$
$(-D, D, 0)$	$(135^\circ, 90^\circ)$
$(-D, D, -D)$	$(135^\circ, 135^\circ)$
$(0, 0, D)$	$(-, 0^\circ)$

In the implemented algorithm, an offset distance $D = 1$ between adjacent pixels has been considered, obtaining 13 3D co-occurrence matrices for the entire hyperspectral cube. The diagonal elements of such matrices represent pixel pairs with no gray level difference and contain information on clusters of

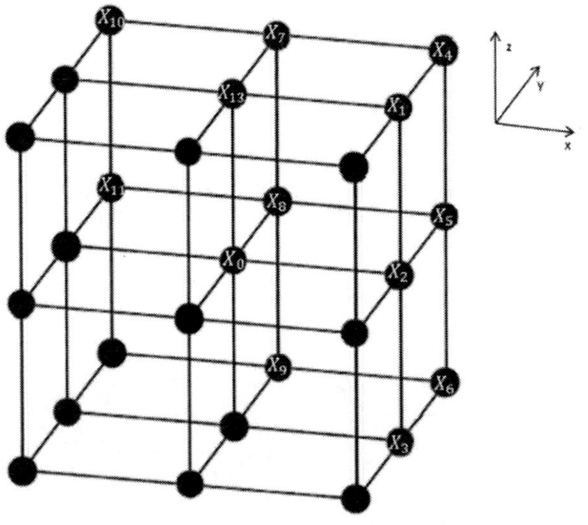

Figure 2. Pixel of interest X_0 and the adjacent pixels in the 13 allowed directions.

pixels. Then, for each matrix, the following operations were performed:

1) extraction of the main diagonal;
2) computation of the histogram of the values of the main diagonal;
3) detection of the local maximum of the histogram.

The gray value corresponding to the local maximum is an index of the number of clusters present in the considered co-occurrence direction, therefore the total number of clusters of the hyperspectral image is obtained as the maximum value among the 13 local maxima.

B. ROIs detection

After the identification of the K clusters, the various spectral signatures represented by the centroid vector are computed and remain saved in the on-board memory. Since data are not normally distributed, these classes are statistically discriminated through two nonparametric quantities: the median value and the interquartile range. These parameters are also used to specify the ROIs by the user.

In order to identify practical regions of interest, a rectangular window of fixed size is chosen to circumscribe the identified clusters. Therefore, a rectangular and fixed-size block is applied to the scanning of the image. Every time the window selects a region where the cluster of interest is in majority (i.e., over a given threshold), the rectangle is classified as ROI, else it is classified as background. The coordinates of the ROIs are saved for the recognition of these regions in the various spectral bands of the original image.

C. ROIs encoding

The DWT is often used in image processing applications and for compression. It is a decomposition f signals into lower resolution and details and it may be viewed as successive low-pass and high-pass filtering of a discrete time-domain signal. On the selected regions of interest, a 2D-DWT is performed for each band. If the considered image for a given band is composed by A rows and B columns, after the 2D-DWT operation, four sub-bands (C,H,D,V) images, each with A/2 rows and B/2 columns, are obtained. The sub-band C has the highest energy compared to the other sub-bands, since it corresponds to the low-pass horizontal and vertical coefficients of the wavelet transform. The 2D-DWT of a function $g(x,y)$ of size $A \times B$ is:

$$W_\delta(a,b) = \frac{1}{\sqrt{AB}} \sum_{y=0}^{B-1} \sum_{x=0}^{A-1} g(x,y)\delta_{a,b}(x,y) \qquad (2)$$

$$W_\vartheta^k = (j,a,b)\frac{1}{\sqrt{AB}} \sum_{y=0}^{B-1} \sum_{x=0}^{A-1} g(x,y)\vartheta_{j,a,b}^k(x,y) \qquad (3)$$
$$k = H, D, V$$

$$\begin{aligned} \delta_{a,b}(x,y) &= \delta(x-a)\delta(x-b) \\ &= \sum_m h_\delta(m-2a)\sqrt{2}\delta(2x-m) \\ &\times \sum_n h_\delta(n-2b)\sqrt{2}\delta(2x-n) \end{aligned} \qquad (4)$$

$$\begin{aligned} \vartheta_{j,a,b}^H &= 2^{\frac{j}{2}}\vartheta^H(2^j x - a, 2^j x - b) \\ &= 2^{\frac{j}{2}} \sum_m h_\vartheta(m-2a)\sqrt{2}\vartheta(2^{j+1}x - m) \\ &\times \sum_n h_\vartheta(n-2b)\sqrt{2}\vartheta(2^{j+1}x - n) \end{aligned} \qquad (5)$$

where δ is a scaling function, $W_\delta(a,b)$ the approximation coefficients of the function $g(x,y)$, $W_\vartheta^k(j,a,b)$ the coefficients relative to the horizontal, diagonal and vertical details, h_ϑ and h_δ are called wavelet filters. In this work, we have used a biorthogonal wavelet filter [7] [8] after the verification that this wavelet is able to reduce the distortion in the final images, consequent to the approximation in using just the low-pass coefficients.

The block for the the DWT implementation is followed by an operation of uniform scalar dead-zone quantization (USDZQ) [9], in which each component C of each ROI, in relation to the priorities set by the user, is quantized with a different number of bits, which is anyway smaller than that of the original acquisition. The quantization indices are expressed as:

$$q[i] = \text{sign}(C[i]) \lfloor \frac{|C[i]|}{\Delta} \rfloor \qquad (6)$$

where $C[i]$ denotes the samples of sub-band C and Δ is the quantization step.

The rectangular windows (actually, the low-pass coefficient of the wavelet transform), after the identification of the assigned label (ROI or background, if just two level of priority are given) are quantized with a number of bits per pixel (bpp). The ROI are quantized with a number of bits per sample larger than the background windows.

For each quantized window an entropic coding is applied to decrease the length of the code to be transmitted to the ground. Entropy encoding is a variable-length encoding that reduces the volume of data to be transmitted by eliminating, in principle, all the redundancy. In this way, the average number of bits per sample becomes very close to the theoretical limit, i.e., the source entropy [10]:

$$H(P) = \sum_{k=1}^{n} -p(k) \log_2 p(k) \quad (7)$$

where $p(k)$ is the probability of emission of symbol x_k.

In this case, the Huffman encoding [11] has been implemented. Huffman encoding is used for lossless data compression; it is based on the frequency of occurrence of the data. The principle is to use a lower number of bits to encode the data that occur more frequently. The average length of a Huffman code depends on the statistical frequency with which the source produces each symbol from its alphabet. Pixels within a region that must be encoded may be considered as the outcome of a discrete source, according to the fact that their values are outputs of a finite dictionary, since a previous fine quantization has been applied to the image [12]. For a fast implementation, the frequency of all pixels taken from all bands is used to estimate the probability of each symbol. As shown in [13], the Huffman encoding needs less execution time than the other entropy encoding algorithms.

The decoding is performed through the reverse operations of encoding, quantization and 2D-DWT for each ROI and background. The information sent to the decoder, in addition to the entire coded image, are: the coordinates of the ROIs identified with the clustering algorithm, the components (H, D, V) relating to the DWT transform for each ROI and the dictionaries for each ROI and BG used in the Huffman encoding.

III. RESULTS

The purpose of this section is to show an example of unsupervised classification (clustering) of a harbor area followed by the compression of the ROIs to detect the ships near the monitored area in real time.

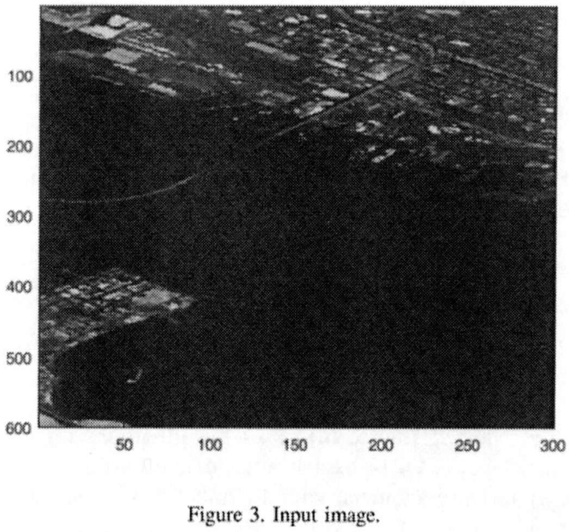

Figure 3. Input image.

An hyperspectral data set acquired by the sensor AVIRIS (mounted on airborne) [14], has been used to test the algorithm. It has 224 contiguous spectral channels with wavelengths from 400 to 2500 nanometers and covers a harbor area of San Diego (USA), as shown in Figure 3. Some bands of the spectrum in which the water vapor absorption is high, have been eliminated so the final extracted hyperspectral image has size 600×300 pixels with 181 bands. In each band, the reported value represents the spectral radiance.

Performing the method described in Section II-A, a number of classes $k = 5$ have been identified. The resulting clustered image is shown in Figure 4. It is important to note that the clustering of the image can be executed just one time, during the first monitoring of a given area.

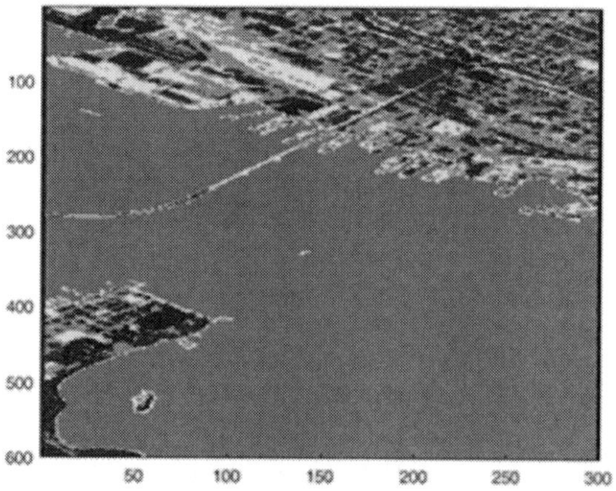

Figure 4. Result after the clustering algorithm.

The spectral signatures relating to the sea, cement and asphalt are supposed to be set by the user and stored in memory, with their median and IQR values. A rectangular window of size 100×100 pixels slides on the clustered image and the algorithm computes the number of pixels belonging to each class within the block window.

A block is classified as ROI if the pixels belonging to the "class sea" occupy from 10% to 90% of the total area and those belonging to "cement" and "asphalt" occupy from 2% to 40% (these values have been calculated through some experimental trials). Four ROIs have been identified whose coordinates are stored and sent to the decoder for a proper reconstruction. The rest of the image, not identified as ROI, is considered background. The bit rate to associate to ROIs and the bit rate to associate to the background have been estimated after an optimization procedure. Initially the maximum value of bpp is taken and then a series of combinations is considered, selecting the best one on the basis of the minimum distortion effect on the ROIs. The results in terms of entropy using different bpp combinations for each ROI, are shown in Table II.

A distortion measure commonly used to evaluate the compressed image quality compared to the original one is the distortion index (DI), defined as:

$$DI = \frac{1}{\frac{1}{ABZ} \sum_{x=0}^{A} \sum_{y=0}^{B} \sum_{z=0}^{Z} [I_{or}(x,y,z) - I_{rec}(x,y,z)]^2} \quad (8)$$

TABLE II. ENTROPY VALUES FOR EACH IDENTIFIED ROI

ROI1 bpp	ROI2 bpp	ROI3 bpp	ROI4 bpp	BG bpp	Entropy-ROI1	Entropy-ROI2	Entropy-ROI3	Entropy-ROI4	Entropy-BG
6	6	6	6	4	2.6756	2.4787	2.1821	3.2062	1.5267
10	10	10	10	4	6.0831	5.7822	5.4600	6.9111	1.5267
12	12	12	12	4	8.0538	7.7570	7.4218	8.9016	1.5267
12	12	12	12	10	8.0538	7.7570	7.4218	8.9016	5.9627

Where A, B, Z represent the three dimensions of image, I_{or} is the original image and I_{rec} is the reconstructed image. Figure 5 shows the results obtained in terms of distortion index and transmitted data volume, in several cases of compression. To make a comparison, the standard JPEG2000 has been applied to the same image. As shown, there is a considerable difference in the distortion level between the implemented method and JPEG2000 compression. This difference can be explained by the fact that the distortion has been calculated only in the region of interest, instead of averaging the result of the distortion that would occur between the ROIs and the BG. The reason of this choice is that the comparison would be otherwise unfavorable to the proposed framework, but at the same time it would be not consistent with the purpose of the algorithm, i.e., the transmission of a reduced data volume to the ground. From the two curves in Figure 5 it is possible to note that, for the same distortion index, the data volume to be transmitted to the Ground Station with the implemented method applied to the ROI is much lower than that obtained with JPEG2000. On the other hand, a drawback of the algorithm is that it compress the part of the image that is not of interest to the user (BG) with a low quality level.

In Figure 6, it is shown an example of reconstructed image (for the 50 band), where the four ROIs are quantized with 10 bpp and the background with 4 bpp.

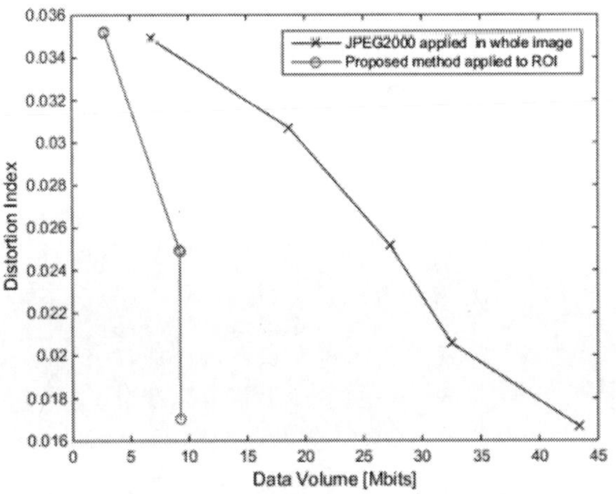

Figure 5. Relationship between data volume and distortion index in JPEG200 (blue) and the proposed method (red).

IV. CONCLUSIONS

The proposed method allows a reduction of the on-board data volume produced by an hyperspectral acquisition system and a better distortion index, at least in the regions of interest, when compared to existing systems in use (e.g., JPEG2000).

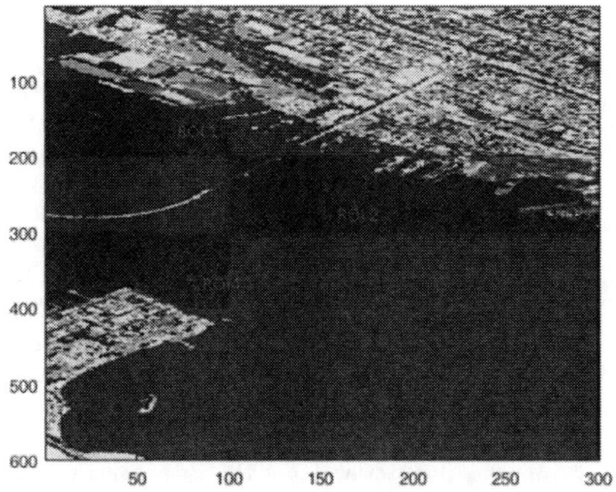

Figure 6. Reconstructed image (relating to 50 band of the cube), 10 bpp for ROIs and 4 bpp for background

These features make the algorithm suitable for real- time (or near real-time) detection of events and recognition of targets. This system works by performing three principal steps:

1) a clustering algorithm that automatically segments the image;
2) an user-oriented choice of the segments and, through this choice, the identification of ROIs;
3) a simpler and faster compression algorithm than the JPEG2000. This is a ROI-based method and it uses wavelet transform and entropy encoding.

To improve the general framework, future developments could include:

- automatic selection of some critical parameters such as the proper number of bits per pixel for ROIs and BG;
- parallelization of the algorithm and its implementation on a Graphic Processor Unit (GPU).
- tests in different scenarios, such as fast identification of oil spills and detection of emergency situations.

ACKNOWLEDGMENT

The research has been carried on in partnership with industrial companies, in the framework of the National Research Project (PON) "Apulia Space", ID $PON03PE\_00067\_6$.

REFERENCES

[1] H .F. Grahn and P. Geladi, Techniques and Applications of Hyperspectral Image Analysis Chichester, U.K.: Wiley, 2007.

[2] S. Mallat, A Wavelet Tour of Signal Processing, San Diego, CA: Academic, 1998.

[3] D. S. Taubman and M. W. Marcellin, JPEG2000: Image Compression Fundamentals, Standards, and Practice, Kluwer, 2001.

[4] A. K. Jain, M. N. Murty, and P. J. Flynn, "Data clustering: a review," ACM Computing Surveys, Vol. 31(3), 1999, pp. 264-323.

[5] K. Koonsanit, and C. Jaruskulchai, "A simple estimation the number of classes in satellite imagery," ICT and Knowledge Engineering (ICT & Knowledge Engineering), 2011 9th International Conference on IEEE, January 2012, pp. 124-128.

[6] A. S. Kurani, D. H. Xu, J. Furst, and D. S. Raicu, "Co-occurrence matrices for volumetric data," 7th IASTED International Conference on Computer Graphics and Imaging, Kauai, USA, August 2004, pp. 447-452.

[7] A. Cohen, I. Daubechies, and J. C. Feauveau, "Biorthogonal bases of compactly supported wavelets," Commun. Pure and Appl. Math., Vol. 45(5), May 1992, pp. 485-560.

[8] M. Antonini, M. Barlaud, P. Mathieu, and I. Daubechies, "Image coding using wavelet transform," IEEE Trans. Image Process., Vol. 1(2), Apr.1992, pp. 205-220.

[9] J. Yu, "Advantages of Uniform Salar Dead-Zone Quantization in Image Coding, Communications, Circuits and Systems," ICCCAS 2004, Vol.2, June 2004, pp. 805-808.

[10] C. E. Shannon, "A mathematical theory of communication," ACM SIGMOBILE Mobile Computing and Communications Review, Vol. 5(1), 2001, pp.3-55.

[11] D. A. Huffman, "A method for the construction of minimum-redundancy codes," Proceedings of the IRE, Vol. 40(9), 1952, pp. 1098-1101.

[12] M. Mitzenmacher, "On the Hardness of Finding Optimal Multiple Preset Dictionaries," IEEE Transaction on Information Theory, Vol. 50(7), July 2004, pp. 1536-1539.

[13] A. Shahbahrami, R. Bahrampour, M. S. Rostami, and M. A. Mobarhan, "Evaluation of Huffman and Arithmetic Algorithms for Multimedia Compression Standards," International Journal of Computer Science, Engineering and Applications (IJCSEA), Vol. 1, August 2011, pp. 34-47.

[14] National Aeronautics and Space Administration (NASA). Airborne visible/infrared imaging spectometer (aviris), retrieved: February, 2016. URL http://aviris.jpl.nasa.gov/

Uncompressed Full HD Video Transmission using Uncoded OFDM over Multipath Fading Channels at 60 GHz

Rodolfo Gomes and Rafael F. S. Caldeirinha[1,2]

[1]Faculty of Computing, Science and Engineering,
University of South Wales,
United Kingdom
[2]Instituto de Telecomunicações (DL-IT),
ESTG, Polytechnic Institute of Leiria,
Leiria, Portugal
Emails: rodolfo.gomes@southwales.ac.uk
and rafael.caldeirinha@ipleiria.pt

Akram Hammoudeh

Faculty of Computing, Science and Engineering,
University of South Wales,
United Kingdom
Email: akram.hammoudeh@southwales.ac.uk

***Abstract*—This paper presents a detailed analysis of the impact of channel impairments on the performance of a mm-Wave wireless uncoded Orthogonal Frequency Division Multiplexing (OFDM) architecture system based on IEEE 802.15.3c standard, for high data-rate applications. The performance of OFDM is known to be severely affected by multipath fading channel when its excess delay exceeds the time guard interval of the OFDM symbol. Hence, this paper analyses the impact of uncompressed Full HD video content transmission over various radio propagation environments suggested by the standard. The impact of the propagation channel impairments is evaluated through appropriate metrics based on Bit Error Rate (BER) and Peak Signal-to-Noise Ratio (PSNR) analysis for residential, office and kiosk scenarios under Line-Of-Sight (LOS) and Non-Line-Of-Sight (NLOS). The feasibility of real-time high-definition video transmission using 60 GHz radio systems will be demonstrated through a proof-of-concept test, which will allow one to perfectly understand the system limitations, and consequently the range of applications that might be developed.**

Keywords–OFDM; Multipath Fading channels; RF-impairments; IEEE 802.15.3c; mmWave signals.

I. Introduction

Communication systems at 60 GHz have recently attracted a great deal of interest allowing multi-gigabit transmission rates. However, radio communications at these frequencies are characterized to yield high free space path losses and thus limited radio coverage. Hence, the target applications or usage models at 60 GHz are mainly short-range indoor applications [1]. In fact, this is an advantage for indoor applications, since the high free space loss in addition to high attenuation by walls, furniture and other objects increases the possible frequency re-use density [2]. Therefore, co-channel interference is reduced and, consequently, it enables a more simplified radio network planning in such environment scenarios.

The IEEE 802.15.3c [3] standard has been created by the IEEE 802.15.3c Task Group 3c (TG3c) [4] as the Wireless Personal Area Network (WPAN) standard for the 60 GHz band, ranging from 57-66 GHz in Europe [5]. As data capacity is ultimately tied to modulation bandwidth, the date rates required for High Definition Multimedia Interface (HDMI) for uncompressed video/audio streaming and for multi-gigabit file transfers are finally met for the first time by standard [5]. Also, the high quantities of information inherent to, e.g., medical image and video, as well as the latency free required transmission, only by means of uncompressed video transmission, demands the utilisation of mmWave in conjunction with protocol independent and processing free information paths. Thus, using 60 GHz millimetre wave band provides the necessary bandwidth and pace for future HD systems.

To this extent, the IEEE 802.15.3c Task Group 3c has proposed a Audio-Visual mode (AV-PHY), where OFDM has been adopted due to its inherent higher bandwidth efficiency [6] and relatively low complexity. An OFDM system is well known to be an effective anti-multipath technique. The latter is primarily due to its reduced channel equalization complexity in the frequency domain due to a single-tap Frequency Domain (FD) equalizer and increased time of transmitted symbol, ain addition to the orthogonality properties between subcarriers [6]. On the other hand, in a single carrier system, the transmitted time symbol is the inverse of the system bandwidth, which means that for multi-gigabit data rates the symbol time becomes very short. This fact leads to a much more complex receiver, i.e., a time-domain equalizer with hundred of taps [7].

In this paper, the reliability of an uncoded OFDM wireless communication system to transmit uncompressed video content at 60 GHz, based on the IEEE 802.15.3c standard [3], under the presence of propagation channel impairments, is assessed. The multipath fading channel models considered are the ones suggested by TG3c [4] for office, residential and kiosk indoor environments, considering both LOS and NLOS scenarios. Moreover, in order to ensure a relatively low system complexity, Zero Forcing (ZF) equalizer is considered and Forward Error Correction Coding (FEC) is not employed. For example in [8], it is shown that using Low Density Parity Check Codes (LDPC) improves the system performance by about 8 to 9 dB at the expense of system complexity and throughput.

The paper is organized as follows. Section II presents the work proposed by the IEEE 802.15.3c Task Group 3c (TG3c) on the 60 GHz channel modeling. Section III introduces

OFDM and its parameters in the system design. The details about the proposed mm-Wave framework are presented in Section IV. Finally, Section V provides results of the performed analysis.

II. INDOOR CHANNEL MODELLING AT 60 GHZ

This section presents the channel modeling [4] proposed by TG3c at 60 GHz for the following indoor environments: office, residential and kiosk. These channel models are based on a frequency sweep technique performed using a Vector Network Analyzer (VNA) to measure the frequency response of the radio channel. The centre frequency and the bandwidth considered in these measurements were 62.5 GHz and 3 GHz, respectively. For each environment, both LOS and NLOS scenarios were considered, except in the kiosk environment, where only LOS has been considered. In such indoor scenarios, multipath components are mainly obtained from reflected or scattered signals from furniture, floor and ceiling.

A. Considered Power Delay Profiles

The IEEE 802.15.3c standard has adopted the generic Complex Impulse Response (CIR) based on the clustering of propagation phenomena in both time and spatial domains, as observed in measurement data [4]. The cluster model is based on the extension of the Saleh-Valenzuela (S-V) model [9] to the angular domain by Spencer [10]. Hence, the IEEE 802.15.3c channel modeling group [11] proposed a statistical channel model dependent on the temporal and spatial domains, where signals arrive at the receiver first in a LOS component, calculated with a two-ray model, and then in clusters (modified S-V model). This 60 GHz channel modeling is utilized in this work, allowing the performance evaluation of OFDM systems over different multipath environments. Additionally, each indoor environment has been mapped onto a channel model and scenario, as presented in Table I.

Table I maps the environment to the channel model and scenario [1].

TABLE I. MAPPING OF ENVIRONMENT TO CHANNEL MODEL AND SCENARIO.

Environment	Channel Model	Scenario
Residential	CM1	LOS
	CM2	NLOS
Office	CM3	LOS
	CM4	NLOS
Kiosk	CM9	LOS

Several channel realizations may be considered to yield different power delay profiles (PDP) for the same multipath environment. This occurs due to the fact that the considered channel modeling tool [11] takes into account the uniform distribution in terms of the scatters movements between transmitter (TX) and receiver (RX) and at different antennas height. Consequently, CIR of each channel model is obtained from 100 quasi-static realizations. Moreover, the PDP has been analyzed in terms of averaged RMS delay spread ($\bar{\tau}_{RMS}$), coherence bandwidth for signal correlation of 0.9 ($\bar{B}_{c_{0.9}}$) and Rician factor ($\bar{K}$). The B_c is a key metric involved in expressing the performance of any digital wireless system over fading channels, where a system bandwidth smaller than the coeherence bandwidth of the channel is required to be considered a flat-fading channel. Otherwise, the fading channel is considered frequency-selective, making the digitally modulated data experiencing Inter-Symbol Interference (ISI) and, thus, higher BER. Coherence bandwidth is normally defined as the maximum frequency difference at which two signals are highly correlated and a correlation of 0.9 ($B_{c_{0.9}}$) is most commonly used. It has been calculated by (1), which is inversely proportional to $\bar{\tau}_{RMS}$ [12].

TABLE II. STATISTICAL PARAMETERS FOR EACH MULTIPATH CHANNEL ENVIRONMENT.

CM #	$\bar{\tau}_{rms}$ (ns)	$\bar{\tau}_{max}$ (ns)	$\bar{B}_{c_{0.9}}$ (MHz)	$\bar{K}$ (dB)	HPBW° (TX/RX)
1	3.547	67.42	5.64	14.6	(360,15)
2	2.73	68.9	7.33	-	
3	22.75	464	0.88	14.61	(30,30)
4	57.7	651	0.35	-	(30,15)
9	2.7	183	7.41	30.9	(30,30)

$$\bar{B}_{c_{0.9}} = \frac{1}{50\bar{\tau}_{RMS}}, \tag{1}$$

Channel quality indicator values of each model are presented in Table II, where HPBW is the Half Power Beamwidth of T_X/R_X antennas.

III. ORTHOGONAL FREQUENCY DIVISION MULTIPLEXING AND SINGLE CARRIER FREQUENCY DOMAIN EQUALIZATION

OFDM is a well known multi-carrier transmission scheme that is mostly used to provide high-data rate links in frequency-selective channels [6]. At the transmitter, a high-rate data stream is transformed into N_c low-rate parallel streams allocated to different orthogonal carriers that can be easily equalized in the frequency domain due to the orthogonality among all those sub-carriers. OFDM can be seen as a multiplexing technique since the output signal is the linear sum of modulated subcarrier signals.

The discrete expression of (2) is given by [6]:

$$x(mT_s) = \sum_{n=0}^{N_c-1} X_n e^{j2\pi nm/N}, \tag{2}$$

where, X_n, n = 0,1,..., N_c-1, is the N_c data symbols corresponding to a two-dimensional QAM constellation.

From (2), it is verified that the discrete OFDM version is an Inverse Fast Fourier Transform (IFFT) operation, which maps the data symbols into adjacent sub-carriers. In the receiver, the Fast Fourier Transform (FFT) is used to demodulate the data symbols.

Although OFDM allows increased time symbol duration for high data rate transmission in comparison with single carrier transmission schemes, the overlapping of OFDM symbols due to multipath effects still has an important impact on system performance. This fact results in the loss of orthogonality among sub-carriers, which severely increases ISI and BER performance. To overcome this issue, a Cyclic Prefix (CP) is introduced and the symbol is cyclically extended from the original harmonic wave of the Fourier period T_s by a guard interval of length T_{CP}. Additionally, the cyclically extended guard interval transforms the convolution of the signal and the channel from linear to a circular convolution and hence a traditional complex time domain equalizer is replaced by a simple single-tap Frequency Domain (FD) equalizer. Moreover, the CP functionality is only efficient when the CP interval time is larger than the maximum delay spread of the multipath channel.

IV. MMWAVE SYSTEM MODELS BASED ON IEEE 802.15.3C STANDARD

The OFDM is implemented based on IEEE 802.15.3c standard, as illustrated in Fig. 1. At the transmitter, a data source is employed to generate pseudo-random bits, which are then mapped into a Gray-coded constellation of QAM symbols. The modulated symbols are mapped into K-subcarriers through K-points IFFT transform. Next, a cyclic extension is inserted. Finally, the wireless channel effect, based on the IEEE model proposed in [4], is taken into account through the convolution of its CIR, presented in subsection II-A, for each channel realization. At the receiver, CIR is ideally estimated and its FFT performed to equalize the received data. Additionally, bit and tone interleaver are used in the OFDM system to enhance its frequency diversity.

In order to shape the OFDM signal Power Spectral Density (PSD), the sub-carriers are allocated into the IFFT according to Table IV [3].

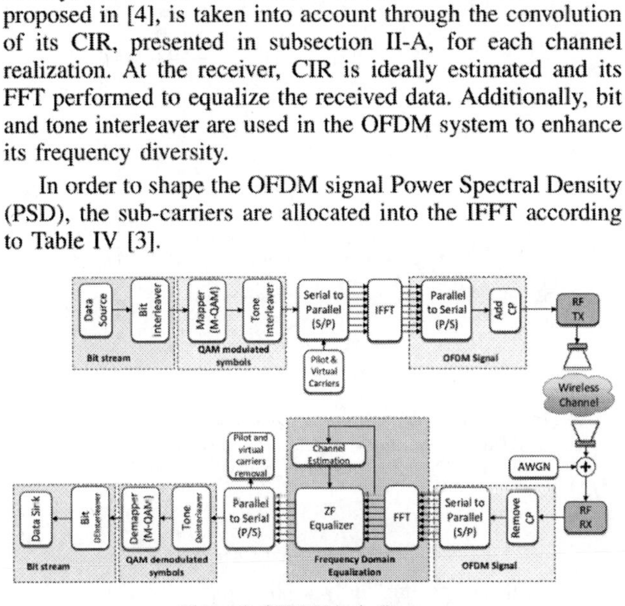

Figure 1. OFDM block diagram.

TABLE III. SUMMARY OF THE MAIN PARAMETERS CONSIDERED IN THE DESIGN OF OFDM SYSTEM BASED ON IEEE 802.15.3C STANDARD.

Parameter	Value
FFT size block (N_{fft})	512
Cyclic prefix (N_{cp})	64 samples
Sampling rate	2640 MHz
Sub-carrier bandwidth	5.15 MHz
Cyclic prefix time (T_{cp})	24.24 ns
Symbol time	218.18 ns
Modulation	16 QAM
Nominal Used Bandwidth	1.815 GHz
Throughput	6.2 Gbps

The data rate requirement to transmit a Full HD video content at a frame rate of 90 Hz and 30 bits per channel per pixel, which are the expected specifications for the next-generation of HDTV [6], is 5.6 Gbps. Therefore, from Table III it is verified that the considered system design provides enough data rate to enable such wireless application.

TABLE IV. SUBCARRIER ALLOCATION IN THE FREQUENCY SPECTRUM DOMAIN.

Subcarrier type	Number of subcarriers	Logical subcarrier indexes
Null	141	[-256:-186]∪[186:255]
DC	3	-1;0;1
Pilot	16	[-166:22:-12]∪[12:22:166]
Guard	16	[-185:-178]∪[178:185]
Data	336	All others

A. Received Signal and Frequency Domain Equalization

The received signal, $y(t)$, after being processed using K-point FFT, is converted into its frequency domain, $Y(k)$. The received OFDM signal, Y_l, considering that $T_{cp} \geq \tau_{max}$ is given by:

$$Y_l(k) = H_l(k).X_l(k) + Z_l(k), \tag{3}$$

where, k^{th} denote the subcarrier frequency component of the lth transmitted OFDM signal, $H_l(k)$ is the Channel Frequency Response (CFR) and $Z_l(k)$ is the AWGN in the frequency domain. The original transmitted information, $X_l(k)$ can be recovered using a Frequency Domain Equalization (FDE) [13], which is performed as a K-branch linear feed-forward equalizer with $C(k)$ being the complex coefficient of the kth subcarrier. In this work, only one FDE approach is considered, namely Zero Forcing (ZF) due to its relatively low implementation complexity, i.e., it does not require signal-to-noise ratio (SNR) estimation. For the ZF criterion, $C(k)$ is defined by (4).

$$C_{ZF}(k) = \frac{\hat{H}(k)^*}{|\hat{H}(k)|^2} \tag{4}$$

where, $\hat{H}(k)$, * and $|.|$ denote the estimated CFR, conjugate transpose and modulus, respectively.

V. EFFECT OF CHANNEL IMPAIRMENTS ON THE OFDM PERFORMANCE

In this section, the uncoded OFDM system performance over the IEEE standard channel model [4] at 60 GHz is assessed using ZF equalization and employing 16 QAM modulation. The quality of the transmitted uncompressed video content in Full HD, is assessed through BER and PSNR analysis. In addition, it is possible to estimate the minimum value of E_b/N_o to ensure a relatively satisfactory subjective quality of the video frame depicted in Fig. 2 used for this purpose. This is achieved by using the relation between the PSNR (objective quality assessment metric) and the subjective quality assessment based on viewer's impression, presented in Table V [14].

TABLE V. RELATION BETWEEN SUBJECTIVE AND OBJECTIVE QUALITY INDICATORS.

PSNR [dB]	ITU Quality scale
> 37	5 - Excellent
$31 - 37$	4 - Good
$25 - 31$	3 - Satisfactory
$20 - 35$	2 - Poor
≤ 20	1 - Very poor

Figure 2. Reference frame from the Full HD Cactus.yuv video sequence for the PSNR calculation.

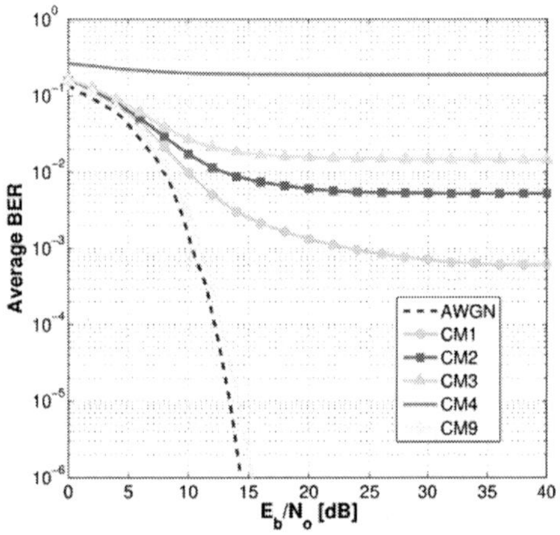

Figure 3. Uncoded OFDM BER performance for various channel models.

The average uncoded OFDM BER results, computed for each channel model, are displayed in Fig. 3. It is evident from these results that the performance of OFDM is severely affected by the propagation channel environment. As depicted only the performance of 16 QAM uncoded OFDM over CM9 meets the recommended BER target for video streaming applications, that is 10^{-6} [4]. This is explained by the fact CM9 is channel model characterized with the highest Rician factor and lowest frequency selectivity. The performance of uncoded OFDM over CM2, CM3 and CM4 environments is relatively poor, since an uncoded OFDM systems are well known to lack of frequency diversity and thus in such radio propagation channels a wireless communication is not reliable. Additionally, CM1 fails to meet the BER target, despite being characterized by a relatively low RMS delay, since CP interval time is shorter than the maximum delay spread of the multipath channel.

In order to evaluate the effectiveness of uncoded OFDM for a relatively good Quality of Service (QoS) at appropriate E_b/N_o values, the degradation of the quality of the video frame for CM9 has been studied. The video frame content (Fig. 2) is divided into several transmitting OFDM symbols and then transmitted over the channel model. PSNR results are depicted in Fig. 4 using 16 QAM, together with those obtained for an ideal radio propagation channel, i.e., no temporal dispersion is presented (dash curve). It be can seen that the effect of CM9 model have not significant impact on the degradation of the quality of reference video frame, with the maximum achievable PSNR of about 60 dB (for a $E_b/N_o = 13$ dB). This characterizes the video frame subjective quality as excellent (Table V).

(a)

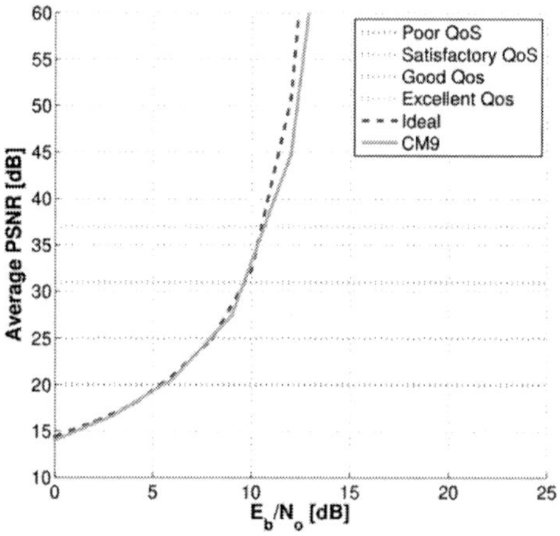

(b)

Figure 4. Video quality performance of the received frame transmitted: a) subject video frame quality at PSNR of 14.01 dB b) objective video frame quality vs E_b/N_o.

VI. Conclusions

In this paper, the study of the impact of channel impairments on a 60 GHz uncoded OFDM system, implemented according to the IEEE 802.15.3c standard, for high data-rate applications, and considering 16 QAM, was presented. The performance assessment of the OFDM system was conducted through BER and PSNR analysis considering the transmission of an uncompressed Full HD video frame over residential, office and kiosk environments, for both NLOS and LOS scenarios.

It has been shown that multipath effect modeled by CM4 induces the largest performance degradation of the system when compared with CM3, CM2 and CM1. It is concluded that the presence of LOS in the multipath scenario is required in a uncoded communication systems, for example it is demonstrated at $E_b/N_o = 40$ dB the maximum BER of OFDM over CM3 is lower than 10^{-3}, whereas at the same E_b/N_o over CM4 the maximum achievable BER is around 0.2. Hence, it is verified that a uncoded 16 QAM OFDM system operating over a relatively low dispersion multipath channel and in a LOS scenario is robust enough to provide a excellent quality of service in streaming uncompressed video for wireless applications. Furthermore, in order to minimize

ISI, for the cases where the BER target is not achieved, FEC coding should be considered at the expense of system complexity and throughput. Apart from CM9 model, no other channel yielded relatively good communication link quality, i.e., the desired BER target was not met for a minimum QoS.

Finally, results presented in this work demonstrate that CM9 is appropriate for low complexity mmWave wireless communication systems envisaged for next generations of HDTV standards, where wireless uncompressed video streaming content is a demand.

REFERENCES

[1] A. Sadri, Summary of the Usage models for 802.15.3c, Nov. 2006.

[2] H. Yang, P. F. M. Smulders, and M. H. A. J. Herben, "Channel Characteristics and Transmission Performance for Various Channel Configurations at 60 GHz," EURASIP J. Wirel. Commun. Netw., vol. 2007, no. 1, Jan. 2007, pp. 43–43.

[3] 802.15.3c-2009 - Physical Layer (PHY) Specifications for High Rate Wireless Personal Area Networks(WPANs).

[4] S. Yong, TG3c Channel Modeling Sub-committee Final Report. Samsung Advanced Institute of Technology, Mar. 2007.

[5] T. Baykas et al, "IEEE 802.15.3c: The First IEEE Wireless Standard for Data Rates over 1 Gb/s," IEEE Communications Magazine, vol. 49, no. 7, July 2011, pp. 114–121.

[6] S. Yong, P. Xia, and A. Garcia, 60 GHz Technology for Gbps. Wiley.

[7] F. Pancaldi et al, "Single-Carrier Frequency Domain Equalization - A Focus on Wireless Applications," IEEE Signal Processing Magazine, Sep. 2008, pp. 1–6.

[8] R. Gomes et al, "Performance and Evaluation of OFDM and SC - FDE over an AWGN Propagation Channel under RF Impairments using Simulink at 60 GHz," in Antennas and Propagation Conference (LAPC), 2014 Loughborough, Nov. 2014, pp. 685–689.

[9] A. Saleh and R. Valenzuela, "A Statistical Model for Indoor Multipath Propagation," IEEE Journal on Selected Areas in Communications, vol. 5, no. 2, Feb. 1987, pp. 128–137.

[10] Q. Spencer, B. Jeffs, M. Jensen, and A. Swindlehurst, "Modeling the statistical time and angle of arrival characteristics of an indoor multipath channel," IEEE Journal on Selected Areas in Communications, vol. 18, no. 3, Mar. 2000, pp. 347–360.

[11] H. Harada et al, CM MATLAB Release Support Document, Mar. 2007.

[12] Y. Choand and W. Yang, MIMO-OFDM Wireless Communications with MATLAB. Wiley.

[13] M. Lei, I. Lakkis, H. Harada, and S. Kato, "MMSE-FDE Based on Estimated SNR for Single-Carrier Block Transmission (SCBT) in Multi-Gbps WPAN (IEEE 802.15.3c)," in IEEE International Conference on Communications Workshops, 2008. ICC Workshops '08, May 2008, pp. 52–56.

[14] H. K. Kim, S.-I. Ao, and B. B. Rieger, IAENG Transactions on Engineering Technologies: Special Edition of the World Congress on Engineering and Computer Science 2011. Springer Science & Business Media, Sep. 2012.

A Method to Separate Musical Percussive Sounds using Chroma Spectral Flatness

F.J. Cañadas-Quesada, P. Vera-Candeas, N. Ruiz-Reyes, A. Muñoz-Montoro, F.J. Bris-Peñalver

Telecommunication Engineering Department, University of Jaen
Scientific and Technological Campus, Cinturon Sur s/n, 23700
Linares, Jaen, Spain

Email: fcanadas@ujaen.es, pvera@ujaen.es, nicolas@ujaen.es, antoniojmmontoro@gmail.com, fjbris@gmail.com

***Abstract*—This paper presents an unsupervised Non-Negative Matrix Factorization (NMF) approach to extract percussive sounds from monaural music signals. Due to unconstrained NMF cannot discriminate between percussive, harmonic or singing-voice components in the decomposition process, we propose a novel method to extract percussive sounds based on the anisotropic smoothness of percussive chroma. Thus, percussive sounds can be discriminate because chroma from percussive sounds clearly draws lines along the chroma. Under a NMF framework, a time-domain signal related to a component is labelled as percussive is the energy distribution of its chroma is approximately flat. This proposal does not require information about the number of active sound sources neither prior knowledge about the instruments nor supervised training to classify the bases. Real-world audio mixtures composed of Harmonic/Percussive and Harmonic/Percussive/Singing-voice sounds were evaluated. Experimental results showed that the proposal was effective compared to state-of-the-art methods. An interesting advantage of the proposal is that it can remove most of the singing-voice components from the extracted percussive signals.**

Keywords–Non-negative matrix factorization; Sound source separation; monaural; percussive; chroma; spectral flatness; distortion;

I. INTRODUCTION

The extraction of percussive sounds from monaural audio mixtures has received much attention over the last decade. Percussive sounds, e.g., snare drum, are impulsive and are typically smooth in frequency. Harmonic sounds, e.g, bass or piano, are quasi-stationary and are typically smooth in time. Therefore, percussive sounds have a structure that is vertically smooth in frequency, whereas harmonic sounds have a structure that is horizontally smooth in time. However, singing-voice sounds are not smooth in frequency because most of them are composed of spectral peaks located at integer multiples of the fundamental frequency and are not smooth in time due to pitch fluctuations (e.g., vibrato effect) as can be seen in Figure 1. Specifically, Figure1 shows that percussive sounds draw vertical lines whereas harmonic sounds draw horizontal lines. Singing-voice sounds draw fluctuated lines over the time. A method capable of separating percussive sounds from audio can be used to facilitate a wide range of Music Information Retrieval (MIR) applications. Some of these include onset detection, beat tracking, rhythm pattern recognition, remixing and for audio to score alignment.

Several approaches have exploited the concept of anisotropic smoothness which is related to the difference in the directions of continuity between the spectrograms of harmonic and percussive sounds. Ono et al. [1] [2] separate harmonic and

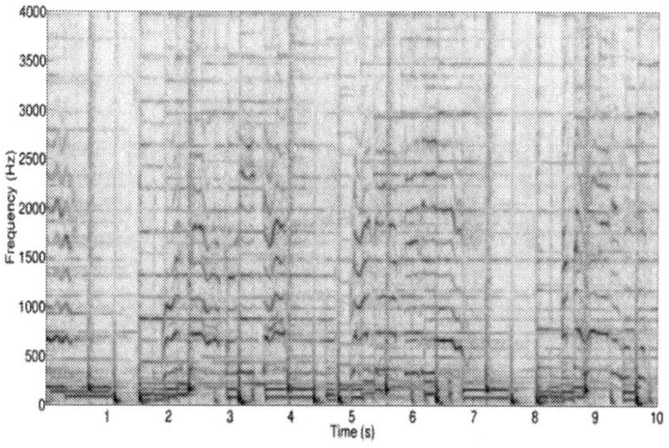

Figure 1. Spectrogram of an audio excerpt composed of percussive, harmonic and singing-voice sounds.

percussive sounds by exploiting the anisotropy of harmonic and percussive sounds in a Maximum A Posteriori (MAP) framework. Fitzgerald's system [3] extracts percussive sounds using the anisotropy smoothness by means of a median filtering. In this manner, the harmonics are considered to be outliers in a temporal slice that contains a mixture of percussive and pitched instruments. In [4], percussive extraction is performed using non-negative matrix partial co-factorization. Thus, the shared basis vectors in this co-factorization are associated with the percussive features, which are used to extract drum-related components from audio.

Recently, a measure [5] based on a segmental spectral flatness is used to distinguish between harmonic and percussive signals. However, evaluation was performed using mixtures composed of one harmonic source and one percussive source not providing experimental results with commercial real-world excerpts. Becker et al. [6] propose an extension that supports spectral continuity and a new temporal continuity constraint using temporal flatness. Canadas et al. [7] propose an unsupervised learning process based on a modified Non-Negative Matrix Factorization (NMF) approach that automatically distinguishes between percussive and harmonic bases by integrating spectro-temporal features, such as anisotropic smoothness or time-frequency sparseness, into the factorization process.

In this paper, we propose an intuitive, novel and fast method to separate percussive sounds from monaural music. Using the concept of anisotropic smoothness, in a similar way as the spectrogram of a percussive sound draws a line along the frequency direction, the chroma of a percussive sound draws a line along the 12 distinct semitones. A time-domain signal related to a component decomposed by NMF can be labelled as percussive if the energy distribution of its chroma is approximately flat.

The remainder of the paper is organized as follows. Section II introduces NMF and its application to sound source separation briefly. Section III describes the proposed method. Experimental results and performance analysis are shown in Section IV. Conclusions and future work are reported in Section V.

II. BACKGROUND

NMF [8] is a technique for multivariate data analysis which aims to obtain a parts-based representation of objects, by imposing non-negative constraints. Given a matrix $\mathbf{X}$ of dimensions $F \times T$ with non-negative entries, it is possible to model it as linear combinations of K elementary non-negative spectra. Therefore, NMF is the problem of finding a factorization:

$$\mathbf{X} \approx \hat{\mathbf{X}} = \mathbf{WH} \tag{1}$$

where $\hat{\mathbf{X}}$ is the estimated matrix, $\mathbf{W} \in \mathbb{R}^{F \times K}$ is the matrix whose columns are the bases, spectral patterns or components. $\mathbf{H} \in \mathbb{R}^{K \times T}$ is a matrix of component gains or activations for all frames. K is usually chosen such that $FK + KT << FT$, hence reducing the data dimension. In typical audio applications, the matrix $\mathbf{X}$ is chosen as a time-frequency representation (e.g., magnitude or power spectrogram), $f = 1, ..., F$ denoting the frequency bin and $t = 1, ..., T$ the time frame.

In the case of magnitude spectra, the parameters are restricted to be non-negative, then, a common way to compute the factorization in Eq. (1) is generally obtained by minimizing a cost function defined as

$$D(\mathbf{X}|\hat{\mathbf{X}}) = \sum_{f=1}^{F} \sum_{t=1}^{T} d(X_{ft}|\hat{X}_{ft}) \tag{2}$$

where $d(a|b)$ is a function of two scalar variables, d is typically non-negative and takes value zero if and only if $a = b$. In this work, the generalized Kullback-Leibler divergence has been used since it is the most frequently used cost function in sound source separation [9] and our preliminary experiments showed that the generalized Kullback-Leibler divergence obtained better separation performance compared to Euclidean distance and the Itakura Saito divergence [10].

An iterative algorithm based on multiplicative update rules is proposed in [8] to obtain the model parameters that minimize the cost function. Under these rules, the generalized Kullback-Leibler divergence $D_{KL}(\mathbf{X}|\hat{\mathbf{X}})$ is non-increasing at each iteration and it is ensured the non negativity of the bases and the gains [8].

$$D_{KL}(\mathbf{X}|\hat{\mathbf{X}}) = \sum_{f} \sum_{t} \mathbf{X}_{ft} \log \frac{\mathbf{X}_{ft}}{\hat{\mathbf{X}}_{ft}} - \mathbf{X}_{ft} + \hat{\mathbf{X}}_{ft} \tag{3}$$

The update rules can be defined as follows,

$$\mathbf{H} \leftarrow \mathbf{H} \odot \frac{\mathbf{W}^T \frac{\mathbf{X}}{(\mathbf{WH})}}{\mathbf{W}^T \mathbf{1}_{F,T}} \tag{4}$$

$$\mathbf{W} \leftarrow \mathbf{W} \odot \frac{\frac{\mathbf{X}}{(\mathbf{WH})} \mathbf{H}^T}{\mathbf{1}_{F,T} \mathbf{H}^T} \tag{5}$$

where $\mathbf{W}$ and $\mathbf{H}$ are initialized as random positive matrices, $\mathbf{1}_{F,T}$ represents a matrix of all-one composed of F rows and T columns, ^{T} is the transpose operator, $\odot$ represents the Hadamard (element-wise) multiplication and the division is also element-wise.

III. PROPOSED METHOD

An intuitive, novel and fast method to extract percussive sounds in music recordings is proposed. It is composed of three stages (NMF, Chroma and Spectral flatness) shown in Figure 2.

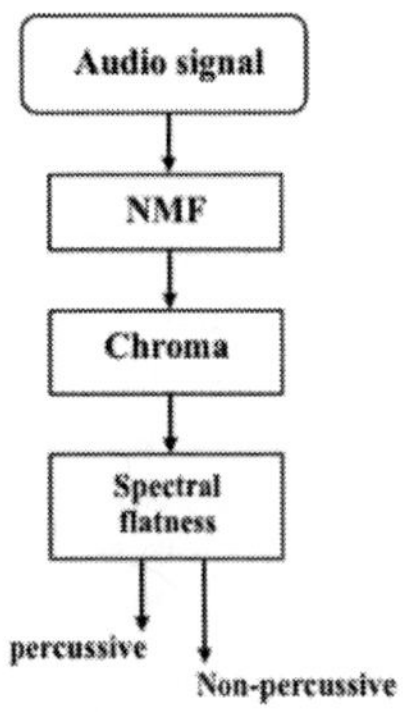

Figure 2. Block diagram of the proposed percussive separation method

The main idea of the proposal is based on the concept of anisotropic smoothness. Instead of using the anisotropic smoothness with the spectrogram data [2] [3], we use the anisotropic smoothness with the chroma data. To obtain the chroma data, a time-frequency representation is used in which the entire spectrum is projected onto 12 bins representing the 12 distinct semitones (or chroma) of the musical octave. As a result, the chroma representation reports the intensity of each of the 12 distinct musical chroma of the octave at each time frame [11]. Just like a spectrogram of percussive sounds draw lines along the frequency direction, Figure 3 shows that chroma of a percussive sound also draws lines along the 12 distinct semitones because percussive sounds are characterized by smoothness in frequency. Therefore, our aim is to classify what components from NMF are percussive using the information provided by the energy distribution of the chroma.

In a first stage, the magnitude of the Short-Time Fourier Transform (STFT) $\mathbf{X}$ of a music signal $x(t)$, with a complex spectrogram $\mathbf{X_c}$ composed of T frames and F frequency bins, is calculated (details are shown in section IV-B). Using the generalized Kullback-Leibler divergence as previously mentioned, an unconstrained NMF is applied to the input spectrogram $\mathbf{X}$ using the update rules Eq. (4)-(5) obtaining a set of K bases or components.

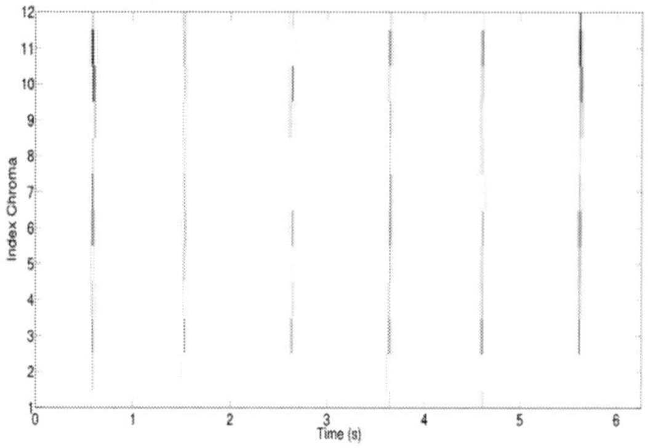

Figure 3. Chroma of a percussive time-domain reconstructed component obtained from NMF. There exists six drum sounds along the time.

In a second stage, each time-domain signal $x_i(t)$ from each component i^{th} is synthesized by the inverse overlap-add STFT of the product of the basis W_i and the activations H_i related to the component i^{th} and using the phase spectrogram of the input signal $x(t)$. Next, the chroma matrix [11] of the signal $x_i(t)$ is calculated generating a sequence of 12 frequency bins and T short-time frames and finally a chroma vector C_i is calculated summing all frames.

Initially, we applied the measure spectral flatness [12] directly on the bases W_i obtained in the NMF decomposition but results showed that it does not work because this measure is very sensitive to small values [5]. In order to overcome this problem, we propose to compute the chroma spectral flatness SF_i because each chroma bin has lower probability of having a small value. The measure chroma spectral flatness SF_i is computed using the measure spectral flatness [12] on the chroma vector C_i instead of basis vector W_i to avoid the high dependency of the spectral flatness related to the small values. $SF_i = 0$ implies a perfect harmonic sound while a $SF_i = 1$ implies a perfect percussive sound.

$$SF_i = \frac{\left(\prod_{k=1}^{12} C_i(k)\right)^{\frac{1}{12}}}{\frac{1}{12}\sum_{k=1}^{12} C_i(k)} \in [0, 1] \qquad (6)$$

Therefore, the extracted percussive signal $x_p(t)$ is the sum of all the signals $x_i(t)$ whose spectral flatness SF_i is higher than a threshold U. In this manner, $x_p(t)$ is composed of all signals $x_i(t)$ whose energy distribution of its chroma is approximately flat.

IV. Evaluation

A. Data set, metrics and State-of-the-art methods

Two data sets T1 and T2, composed of the same nine monaural real-world music excerpts, taken from the Guitar Hero game [13] [14], have been generated to evaluate the proposed method as can be seen in Table I. To perform an objective evaluation, each music excerpt from database T1 was created mixing the original percussive and harmonic instrumental tracks without using any singing-voice track. However, each music excerpt from database T2 was created mixing the same percussive and harmonic instrumental tracks of the database T1 and the original singing-voice track. Each excerpt has a duration about 30 seconds. All of the signals were converted from stereo to mono and sampled at 16 kHz.

TABLE I. IDENTIFIER, TITLE AND ARTIST OF THE FILES OF THE DATABASES T1 AND T2

IDENTIFIER	TITLE	ARTIST
$M1$	Hollywood Nights	Bob Seger & The Silver Bullet Band
$M2$	Hotel California	Eagles
$M3$	Hurts So Good	John Mellencamp
$M4$	La Bamba	Los Lobos
$M5$	Make It Wit Chu	Queens Of The Stone Age
$M6$	Ring of Fire	Johnny Cash
$M7$	Rooftops	Lost prophets
$M8$	Sultans of Swing	Dire Straits
$M9$	Under Pressure	Queen

The assessment of the performance of the proposed method has been performed using the metrics Source to Distortion Ratio (SDR), Source to Interference Ratio (SIR) and Source to Artifacts Ratio (SAR) [15] [16] widely used in the field of sound source separation. Specifically, SDR provides information on the overall quality of the separation process. SIR is a measure of the presence of non-percussive sounds in the percussive signal and vice versa. SAR provides information on the artifacts in the separated signal from separation and/or resynthesis. Higher values of these ratios indicate better separation quality. More details can be found in [15].

We compare the separation performance of the proposed method with two reference percussive and harmonic sound separation methods. The first one is the method HPSS [2] and the second one is the method MFS [3].

B. Parameters

The STFT of each mixture has been calculated using half-overlapping Hamming window of $L = 1024$ samples, corresponding to a duration of 64 milliseconds at a sampling rate of 16KHz [1] [2] [7].

A random initialization of the matrices W and H was used and the convergence of the NMF decomposition was empirically observed which was achieved after 100 iterations. Due to NMF is not guaranteed to find a global minimum, the performance of the proposed method depends on the initial values of NMF [9] leads to different results. For this reason, we have repeated three times for each excerpt and the results in the paper are averaged values.

Highlight that the best separation performance will be obtained using an optimization process which is data dependent because NMF is a blind decomposition method and it is not based on the physics of the problem. As a result, the separated signals from NMF are not independent, nor uncorrelated, it generates many false positives and/or mixing of percussive/non-percussive sounds. In our preliminary results, we have evaluated different numbers of components $K = 10, 20, 30, 40$ and we selected the value $K = 10$ because it obtained the best separation performance. It seems that a small number of components improves the percussive separation because the subspace of percussive sounds is of lower rank compared to harmonic or singing-voice rank [17] [18].

C. Optimization

Figure 4 and Figure 5 show the optimization of the threshold U in the database T1 and T2. A lower value of $U < 0.5$ captures higher percentage of non-percussive sounds that implies a reduction of the percussive SIR. A value around $U = 0.6$ allows a promising discrimination between percussive and non-percussive sounds. The optimum value of the threshold $U_{o1} = 0.6$ in the database T1 and $U_{o2} = 0.7$ in the database T2 have been selected because reach the best percussive and non-percussive SDR and a high percussive SIR associated with the highest non-percussive SIR. This situation reports that the proposed system extracts a high percentage of percussive sounds avoiding the extraction of non-percussive sounds and viceversa. It can be seen that higher values of $U > 0.7$ lose a high amount of percussive sounds that causes a drastically reduction of the non-percussive SIR. Comparing Figure 4 and Figure 5, an optimum threshold $U_{o2} > U_{o1}$ must be set because the system needs to be more strict to separate sounds from singing-voice active in the database T2.

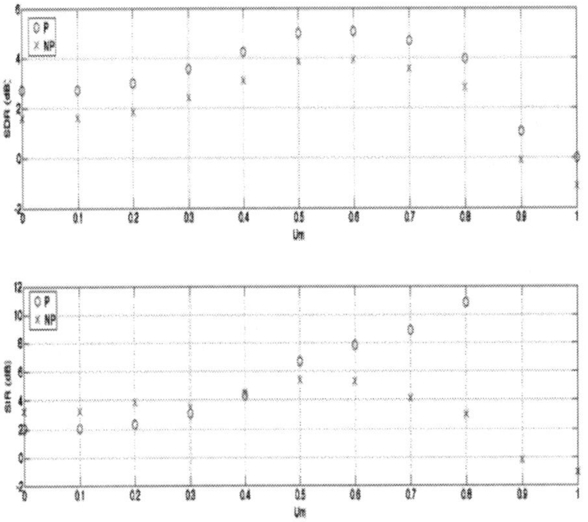

Figure 4. Average SDR-SIR obtained in function of the threshold U_m for the database T1. The legend P is related to percussive results and the legend NP is related to non-percussive results.

The optimum thresholds U_{o2} and U_{o1} will be used in the next section in order to evaluate the performance of the proposed system.

D. Results

Figure 6 and Figure 7 show SDR, SIR and SAR results evaluating the database T1 and T2 for the proposed method and the two state-of-the-art methods. Each box represents nine data points, one for each excerpt of the test database. Each method evaluated shows three boxes in figures. The left box represents the average value of the percussive separation results. The center box represents the average value of the non-percussive (harmonic sounds in the database T1 and harmonic+singing-voice sounds in database T2) separation results. The right box represents the overall average value considering the percussive and non-percussive separation results. The lower and upper lines of each box show the 25th and 75th percentiles for the database. The line in the middle of each box represents the median value of the dataset. The lines extending above and below each box show the extent of the rest of the samples, excluding outliers. Outliers are defined as points that are over

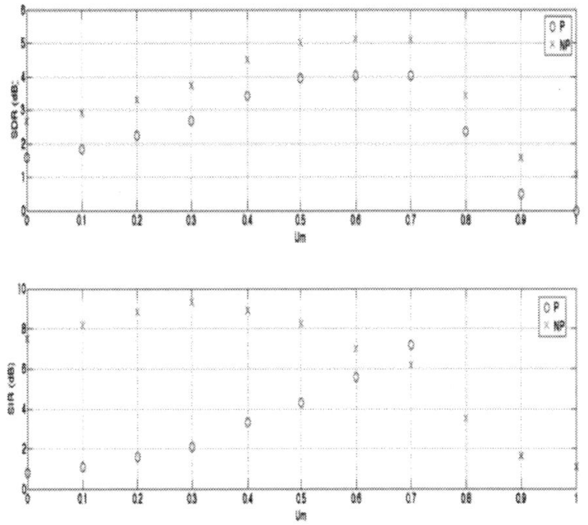

Figure 5. Average SDR-SIR obtained in function of the threshold U_m for the database T2. The legend P is related to percussive results and the legend NP is related to non-percussive results.

1.5 times the interquartile range from the sample median, which are shown as crosses.

Figure 6 displays the SDR separation performance for the database T1. It shows that MFS and the proposed method obtain the best percussive separation performance but HPSS can be considered as competitive method. Moreover, MFS achieves the best SDR taking into account non-percussive and overall separation followed by the proposed method. Taking into account SIR results, HPSS produces the best percussive SIR and MFS provides the best non-percussive SIR. However, the non-percussive SIR of the proposed method is the worst of them. This performance is because not all the bases decomposed by NMF and labelled as percussive are purely percussive bases (ideally, each component represents parts of a single sound source). It implies that some of the non-percussive sounds are also synthesized as percussive sounds by the proposed method. Therefore, the proposed method depends on the randomized initialization of the two matrices W and H in the NMF decomposition. Taking into account SAR results, HPSS achieves a high percussive SIR at the expense of introducing more artifacts, which it can be observed by the worst percussive and harmonic SAR. Nevertheless, the proposed method provides the best percussive and non-percussive SAR results because the artifacts in the reconstruction signal are minimized.

Figure 7 displays the separation performance for the database T2. Hereafter, all the comments are related to the comparison between Figure 6 and Figure 7. It can be observed that the addition of the singing-voice in the non-percussive sounds reduces about 1dB the overall SDR both MFS and HPSS but not in the proposed method. Specifically, the proposed method improves the overall SDR in about 1dB, obtaining approximately the same overall SDR that MFS. While HPSS and MFS reduces its percussive SIR about 5dB, the SIR reduction of the proposed method is only about 0.7dB. This performance indicates that a high amount of singing-voice sounds are active in the separated percussive signals

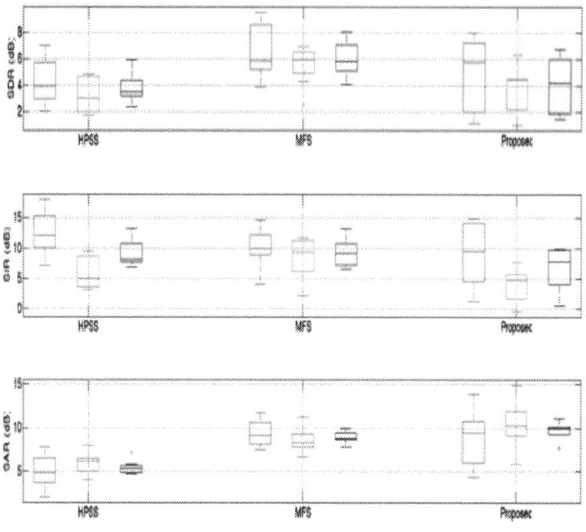

Figure 6. Separation performance in SDR, SIR and SAR results evaluating the database T1. The left box represents the average value of the percussive separation results. The center box represents the average value of the non-percussive separation results. The right box represents the overall average value considering the percussive and non-percussive separation results.

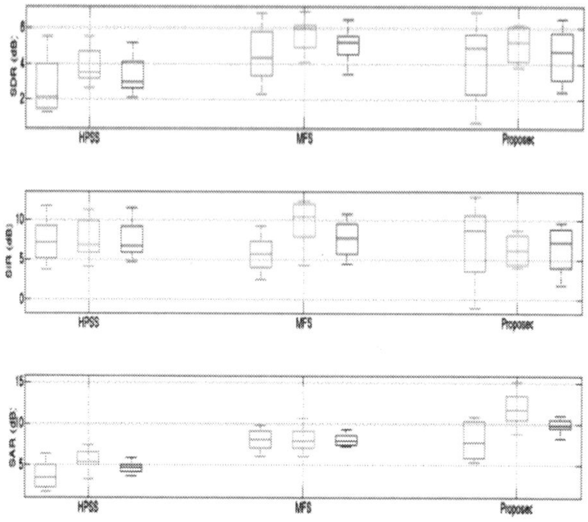

Figure 7. Separation performance in SDR, SIR and SAR results evaluating the database T2. The left box represents the average value of the percussive separation results. The center box represents the average value of the non-percussive separation results. The right box represents the overall average value considering the percussive and non-percussive separation results.

from HPSS and MFS. Moreover, the overall SIR in HPSS and MFS is reduced more than twice compared with the proposed method. As occurred in Figure 6, the proposed method achieves the best SAR results minimizing the artifacts in the reconstruction signal. Therefore, results report a strength of the proposed method, which is not exhibited by the other compared methods, that is the capability to successfully remove the singing voice sounds in the separated percussive signal. This capability implies that the proposed method provides the best tradeoff between the quality of the separated percussive signal and the removal of the singing voice sounds. An example of the mentioned capability to remove the singing voice sounds in the separated percussive signal is shown in Figures 8-10. It can be clearly observed that in the spectral range [400Hz-1600Hz] that most singing-voice sounds, characterized by fluctuated frequencies over the time, have only been removed using the proposed method.

To illustrate the separation performance of the proposed method, some percussive audio examples have been uploaded to a web page [19].

V. Conclusion

A novel, intuitive and fast method to separate percussive sounds from music, composed by percussive/harmonic instruments and singing-voice, is presented. Due to the fact that unconstrained NMF cannot discriminate between percussive, harmonic or singing-voice components in the decomposition process, we propose to extract percussive sounds based on the anisotropic smoothness of chroma. If the energy distribution of its chroma is approximately flat, then a time-domain signal related to a component decomposed by NMF can be labelled as percussive. This proposal does not require prior knowledge about the instruments nor supervised training to classify the bases.

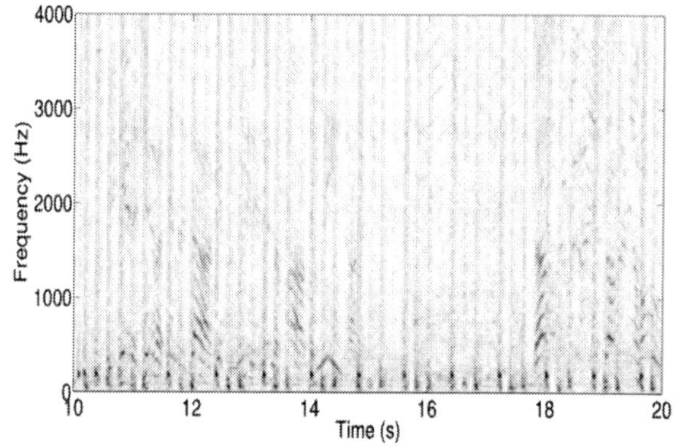

Figure 8. Percussive separation of the method HPSS evaluating the interval [10s-20s] of the file M8 of the database T2. Higher grey level represents higher energy of each frequency.

Although the separation performance of the proposed method is competitive in evaluating mixtures of percussive and harmonic instruments, its performance depends on the randomized initialization of the two matrices W and H in the NMF decomposition. The reason is because not all the bases labelled as percussive from NMF are purely percussive so, non-percussive sounds are also synthesized as percussive sounds by the proposed method. Taking into account mixtures of percussive and harmonic instruments and singing-voice, the proposed method improves the separation performance compared with the other methods. Results show that an advantage of the proposed method, which is not exhibited by the other compared methods, is the capability to successfully remove the singing voice sounds in the separated percussive signal.

Future work will be focused on two topics. First, we

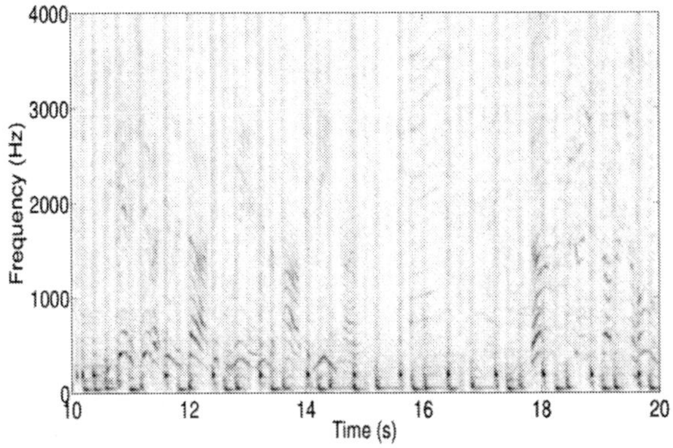

Figure 9. Percussive separation of the method MFS evaluating the interval [10s-20s] of the file M8 of the database T2. Higher grey level represents higher energy of each frequency

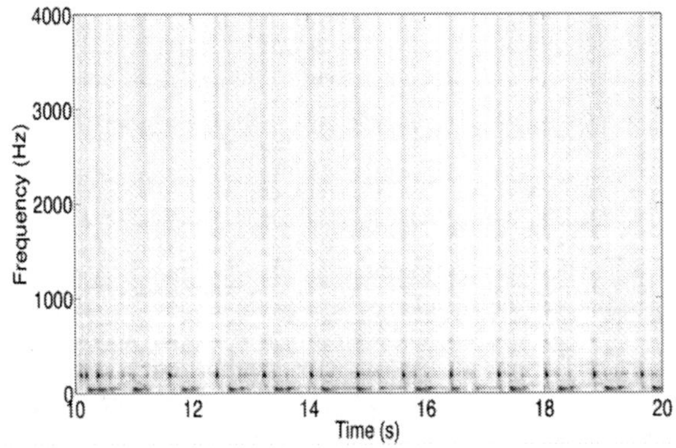

Figure 10. Percussive separation of the proposed method evaluating the interval [10s-20s] of the file M8 of the database T2. Higher grey level represents higher energy of each frequency

will investigate smart initializations based on properties of percussive sounds to improve the quality of the percussive separation. Second, new measures to discriminate the rhythmic accompaniment will be investigated (e.g., bass line).

ACKNOWLEDGMENT

This work was supported by the Andalusian Business, Science and Innovation Council under project P2010- TIC-6762 (FEDER) and the Spanish Ministry of Economy and Competitiveness under Projects TEC2012-38142-C04-01, TEC2012-38142-C04-03 and TEC2012-38142-C04-04.

REFERENCES

[1] N. Ono, K. Miyamoto, H. Kameoka, and S. Sagayama, "A real-time equalizer of harmonic and percussive components in music signals," in Proceedings of the Ninth International Conference on Music Information Retrieval (ISMIR), 2008, pp. 139–144.

[2] N. Ono, K. Miyamoto, J. Le Roux, H. Kameoka, and S. Sagayama, "Separation of a monaural audio signal into harmonic/percussive components by complementary diffusion on spectrogram," in Proceedings of the European Signal Processing Conference (EUSIPCO), 2008, pp. 25–29.

[3] D. Fitzgerald, "Harmonic/percussive separation using median filtering," in Proceedings of Digital Audio Effects (DAFX), 2010, pp. 1–4.

[4] J. Yoo, M. Kim, K. Kang, and S. Choi, "Nonnegative matrix partial co-factorization for drum source separation," in Proceedings of the IEEE International Conference on Acoustics, Speech, and Signal Processing (ICASSP), 2010, pp. 1942–1945.

[5] J. Becker and C. Rohlfing, "A segmental spectral flatness measure for harmonic-percussive discrimination," in Proceedings of International Student Conference on Electrical Engineering, 2013, pp. 1–4.

[6] J. Becker, C. Sohn, and C. Rohlfing, "NMF with spectral and temporal continuity criteria for monaural sound source separation," in Proceedings of European Signal Processing Conference (EUSIPCO), 2014, pp. 316–320.

[7] F. Canadas, P. Vera, N. Ruiz, J. Carabias, and P. Cabanas, "Percussive/harmonic sound separation by non-negative matrix factorization with smoothness/sparseness constraints," Journal on Audio, Speech, and Music Processing, vol. 2014, no. 26, 2014, pp. 1–17.

[8] D. Lee and S. Seung, "Algorithms for non-negative matrix factorization," in Proceedings of Advances in Neural Inf. Process. System, 2000, pp. 556–562.

[9] B. Zhu, W. Li, R. Li, and X. Xue, "Multi-stage non-negative matrix factorization for monaural singing voice separation," IEEE Transactions on Audio, Speech, and Language Processing, vol. 21, no. 10, 2013, pp. 2096–2107.

[10] C. Févotte, N. Bertin, and J. Durrieu, "Nonnegative matrix factorization with the itakura-saito divergence with application to music analysis," Neural Computation, vol. 21, no. 3, 2009, pp. 793–830.

[11] "D. Ellis, Chroma features analysis and synthesis," 2007, URL: http://www.ee.columbia.edu/~dpwe/resources/matlab/chroma-ansyn/ [accessed: 2016-01-02].

[12] A. Gray and J. Markel, "A spectral-flatness measure for studying the autocorrelation method of linear prediction of speech analysis," IEEE Transactions on Acoustics, Speech and Signal Processing, vol. 22, no. 3, 1974, pp. 207–217.

[13] "Activision," 2016, URL: https://es.wikipedia.org/wiki/Guitar_Hero_5 [accessed: 2016-02-02].

[14] "Activision," 2016, URL: https://en.wikipedia.org/wiki/Guitar_Hero_World_Tour [accessed: 2016-02-02].

[15] C. Févotte, R. Gribonval, and E. Vincent., "Bss_eval toolbox user guide - revision 2.0," in Technical report 1706, IRISA, 2005.

[16] E. Vincent, C. Févotte, and R. Gribonval, "Performance measurement in blind audio source separation," IEEE Transactions on Audio, Speech, and Language Processing, vol. 14, no. 4, 2006, pp. 1462–1469.

[17] B. Schuller, A. Lehmann, F. Weninger, F. Eyben, and G. Rigoll, "Blind enhancement of the rhythmic and harmonic sections by nmf: Does it help?" in Proceedings of the 35th German Annual Conference on Acoustics, Acoustical Society of the Netherlands, 2009, pp. 361–364.

[18] Y. Yang, "Low-rank representation of both singing voice and music accompaniment via learned dictionaries," in Proceedings of the 14th International Society for Music Information Retrieval (ISMIR) Conference, 2013, pp. 1–6.

[19] "Audio demo," 2016, URL: https://dl.dropboxusercontent.com/u/22448214/WebSIGNAL2016/indexSIGNAL2016.html [accessed: 2016-04-28].

Time to Digital Converter Transfer Function Improvement using Poisson Process Events

Timothé Turko[1], Anastasia Skilitsi[2], Wilfried Uhring[1], Jean-Pierre Le Normand[1], Norbert Dumas[1], Foudil Dadouche[1], Jérémie Léonard[2]

[1)] ICube, UMR 7357, Université de Strasbourg and CNRS, 23, rue du Loess, 67037 Strasbourg, France

[2)] Institut de Physique et Chimie des Matériaux de Strasbourg & Labex NIE, Université de Strasbourg, CNRS UMR 7504, 23 rue du Loess, 67034 Strasbourg Cedex, France

Email: wilfried.uhring@unistra.fr

***Abstract*— This paper introduces a fast and efficient method to characterize a Time to Digital Converter (TDC) transfer function using Poisson process events. We propose a correction method appropriate for ASIC as well as discrete or FPGA TDCs, to be implemented on a post process unit located after the Time to Digital Converter. We then apply the presented method to a case study that demonstrates the efficiency of the correction by measuring the fluorescence lifetime of a test fluorophore by time-correlated single photon counting (TCSPC) with and without correction. The results show a much nicer signal and better fitting with a 3-fold improvement of the fluorescence lifetime accuracy.**

Keywords - Time to Digital Converter; TDC; Poisson Process; SPAD; Characterization; Correction; Fluorescence Lifetime

I. INTRODUCTION

With the apparition of low cost Single Photon Avalanche Diodes (SPAD) fabricated in standard CMOS technologies, more and more applications based on Time of Flight (TOF) measurements are emerging such as active 3D video cameras [1]. These systems need to measure a precise time duration separating two physical events such as a laser pulse generated by a laser diode and a photon detection event by the SPAD. By TOF measurement, it is possible to deduce the distances traveled by the photon. To measure this fast event duration, Time to Digital Converters (TDCs) are commonly used to convert the physical time information into digital information ready for a processing unit. Several techniques can be employed to design a TDC such as Tapped Delay Line, Delay Locked Loop, Gate Ringed Oscillator, etc. Those functions can be implemented on ASIC or FPGA targets [2].

The TDC transfer function includes some major and/or minor flaws, resulting from conception and/or fabrication defects and uncertainties. Certain elements of the TDC chain are slower or faster than others, resulting in a systematic error that will appear on the transfer function (nonlinearity error, missing bins, etc.). The aim of this paper is to present a characterization method and a simple corrective patch to improve all type of TDCs [3]. It is organized as follows: Section II gives a brief description of the TDC measurement principle, Section III describes the characterization method based on the measurement of Poisson Process Events. A simple correction method is introduced in Section IV and tested in Section V. We demonstrate its efficiency in a case study where the fluorescence lifetime of a fluorophore is determined by time correlated single photon counting (TCSPC) [4] carried out with a FPGA-based TDC.

II. OPERATION PRINCIPLE OF A TDC

A TDC is an electronic system used to measure time intervals between two physical events. The first event generates an electrical signal, which initiates the time measurement. The second event generates a second signal that ends the time measurement.

The time measurement is generally divided in two different processes as shown on Figure 1, corresponding to fine and coarse time scales. First, the first signal starts the coarse measurement that is synchronous with the system clock. The fine measurement is also triggered by the first signal but it is an asynchronous measurement of the time. The fine counter is used to measure with a sub-clock period precision the duration between the signal trigger and the first edge of the clock signal. In order to have the same precision between the stop signal and the last clock edge, a second fine counter is used, see (1). The fine measurement unit is the most critical element of the whole TDC because the time resolution is mainly related to its precision. According to this timing diagram, the total measured time is expressed as follows:

$$T_m = T_{Fine1} + T_{Coarse} - T_{Fine2} = N \cdot T_{clk} + T_{Fine1} - T_{Fine2} \quad (1)$$

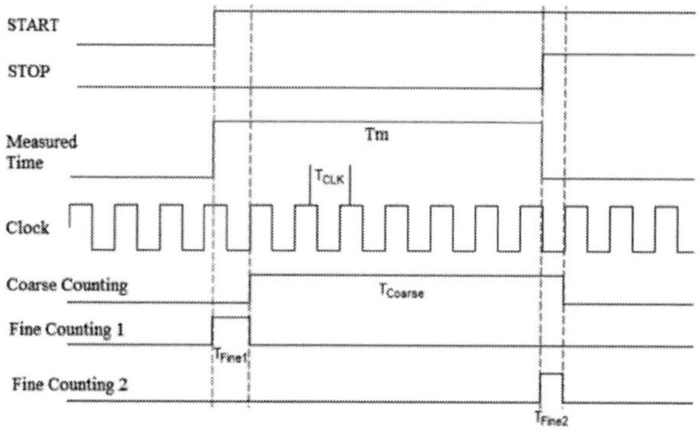

Figure 1. Operation principle of a Time-to-Digital Converter

III. TDC CHARACTERIZATION WITH POISSON PROCESS EVENTS

In order to create a correction method applicable to any type of TDC, the proposed method relies on data post processing. The first step of the proposed method is the characterization of the TDC. The approach consists in measuring a perfectly uniform distribution of temporal events in order to evaluate the accuracy of all TDC bins. Bin accuracy refers to the temporal size of each bin. Indeed, if a bin of the TDC is temporally larger than it should be, it gathers more events from the uniform distribution and thus the total count of this bin is higher. Inversely, a smaller bin shows a total count proportionally lower than expected. A perfect generator of random uncorrelated events is a SPAD that detects photons generated by a "continuous wave" (CW) light source such as a battery-powered Light-Emitting Diode (LED). Indeed, the single photon detection is well known to be an ideal Poisson Process which is completely uniform and uncorrelated.

An ideal TDC should detect the exact same number of photons per time bin, resulting in a flat histogram. If a defect appears on the TDC chain, the error is temporally static. This means that if the measurement is done several times the same error will occur every time and a Fixed Pattern Noise (FPN) will appear on the measured histogram. In addition, due to Poisson statistics, on each measurement, a random noise is added to each bin such that a bin with a value N is affected by a random value equal to $\sqrt{N}$ rms leading to a signal to noise ratio of the bin value also equal to $\sqrt{N}$. Thus one must ensure that the detected FPN is not due to the random noise of the measurement by checking that its value is well above $\sqrt{N}$.

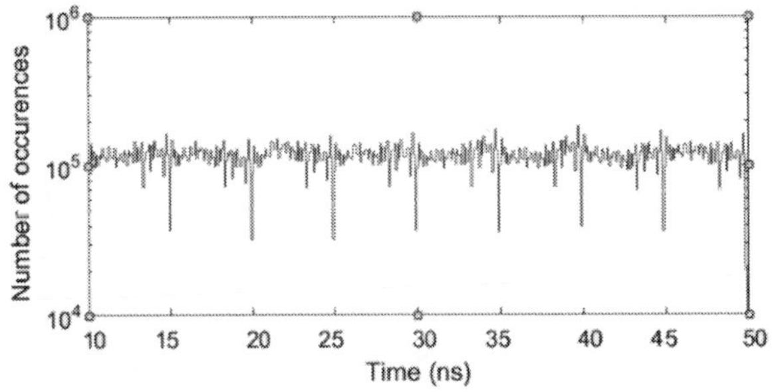

Figure 2. TDC FPN measured over a range of 40 ns by the detection of a large number of non-correlated Poisson events

For example, the histogram displayed in Figure 2 results from a 10 seconds acquisition under a counting rate of 1800 kHz with the FPGA based TDC described in [5] with a temporal resolution of 89 ps over a range of 40 ns. In the specific case of this TDC, the fine counter is a Tapped Delay Line made of 56 elementary delay cells of 89 ps for a total length of 5 ns. This fine TDC counter is thus periodically reinitialized every 5 ns when the coarse counter is incremented. Hence the overall FPN of the TDC is the periodic repetition of the FPN characterizing the 5-ns-long tapped delay line used for the fine TDC counter. Figure 3 displays a zoom on this 5-ns long FPN motif.

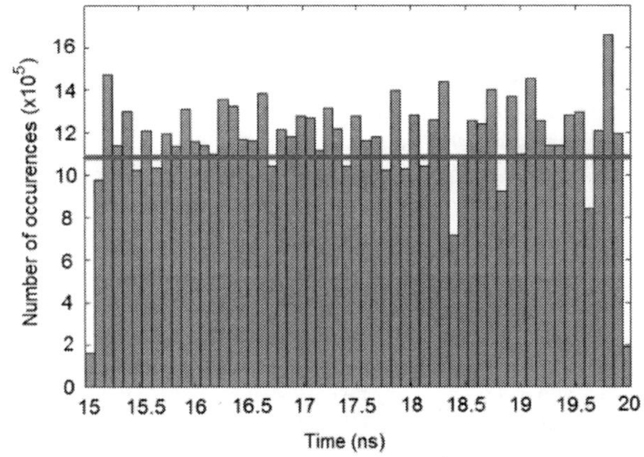

Figure 3. FPN corresponding to the fine TDC counter, periodically repeated every 5ns (coarse counter). Red line indicates the mean bin value.

The overall photon accumulation time is large enough that the uncertainty $\sqrt{N}$ due to Poisson statistic on the average number N of photons per bin becomes much less than the detected variation of N from bin to bin, i.e., the FPN amplitude (see Figure 3). The observed FPN is coming out from the delay mismatch of the tapped delay line used for the fine TDC counter.

Another method for Poisson process events generation using a SPAD is to exploit the photodetector dark count rate originating from thermal activation at ambient temperature. Figure 4 displays the FPN histogram characterizing the fine counter upon accumulating dark counts for over 10 minutes when the SPAD is maintained in pitch dark. The dark count rate is 250 Hz in this case. We note that the FPN is very similar to that of Figure 3, as expected, since it is a property of the TDC, independent of the process (light or dark counts) generating the Poisson distributed events. However, the FPN characterization with a CW light source is much faster (higher counting rate) and therefore preferred. Other light sources like day light and neon light (100 Hz frequency) have been tested yielding the same FPN histogram.

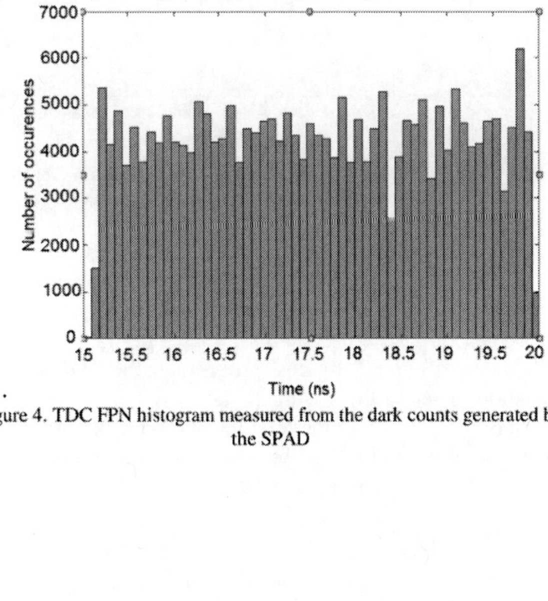

Figure 4. TDC FPN histogram measured from the dark counts generated by the SPAD

The above FPN measurement can be used to retrieve the TDC transfer function without the need of a complex delay generator. As mentioned before, if a bin of the TDC is temporally larger than the mean bin size, its number of counts is correspondingly increased. Consequently, the absolute time TDC transfer function can be extracted from the bin values with:

$$TDC(n) = \frac{T}{M}\frac{1}{\sum_{i=1}^{M} bin_i}\sum_{i}^{n} bin_i \cdot \qquad (1)$$

Where T is the total time range, M is the total number of TDC bins in the time range T. The extracted transfer function of the TDC over the 5-ns time range of the fine counter is presented in Figure 5. The linear fit allows the characterization of the Integral Non Linearity of the TDC. The results obtained with this method are consistent with the measurements reported in [5].

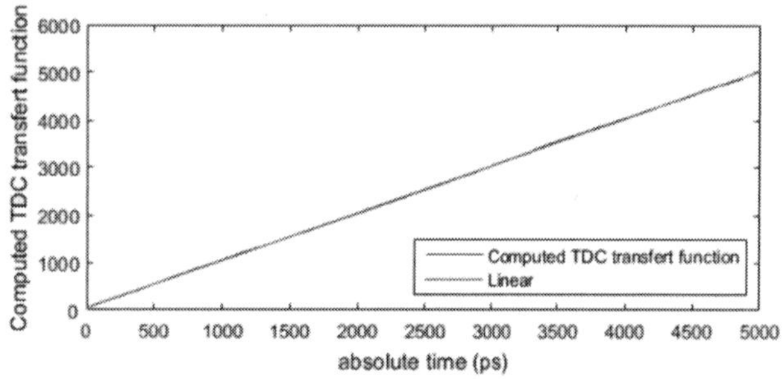

Figure 5,a. Transfer function of the 5-ns long tapped Delay Line of the fine counter of the TDC, characterized with cw light illumination of a SPAD

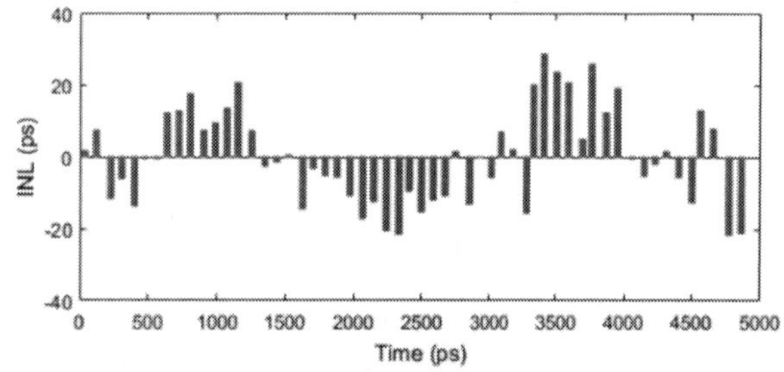

Figure 5,b. INL of the 5-ns long tapped Delay Line of the fine counter of the TDC, characterized with cw light illumination of a SPAD

IV. CORRECTION METHOD

The FPN evidenced in Figure 2 being a systematic bias, it will also affect histograms recorded in TCSPC experiments. Moreover, it can be used to define a scaling factor for each bin so as to correct, by post-processing, the TDC transfer function. This factor is simply the deviation of the count number of each bin_i of the reference FPN histogram relative to the average value (red line in Figure 3), such that the corrected bin count $binc_i$ is given by:

$$binc_i = \frac{\frac{1}{M}\sum_{i=1}^{M} bin_i}{bin_i} \qquad (2)$$

Where M is the total number of TDC bins in the reference FPN histogram. The correction applied to the FPN histogram leads to a completely flat histogram, by construction.

V. CASE STUDY

In the following, the characterized TDC is used in a TCSPC experiment to measure the fluorescence lifetime of fluorescein dissolved in water buffered at pH = 7.4.

A picosecond, 405-nm laser pulse [6] excites the fluorescence. The fluorescence signal is detected by a SPAD and the arrival time of individual photons relative to the previous laser pulse is measured and stored by the TDC on the FPGA board. Figure 6 shows the raw measurement without applying the TDC correction.

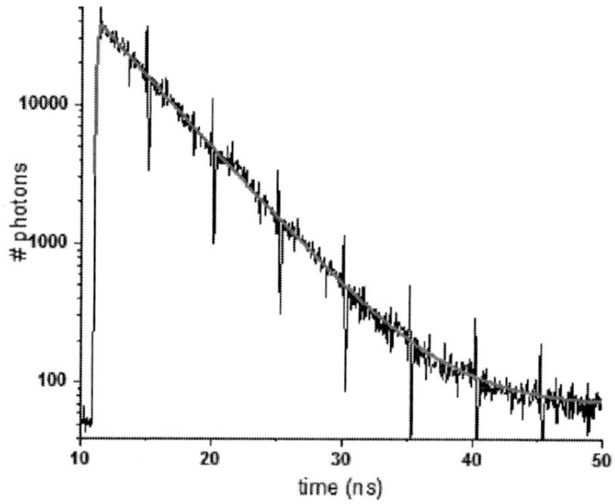

Figure 6. Fluorescence decay without correction

The imperfect transfer function of the TDC creates a static pattern (FPN) at the origin of the periodic glitches in the raw histogram. The 5-ns periodicity of the FPN is clearly seen in this data. The fit to a mono-exponential decay yield a lifetime of 4.21 ns ±0.08 ns.

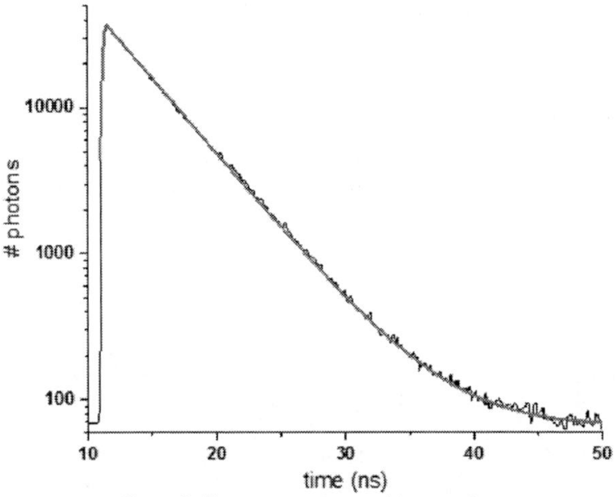

Figure 7. Fluorescence decay with correction

The same data are post-processed by applying to each bin count the correction factor introduced above, and the corrected data are plotted in Figure 7. The FPN is very efficiently attenuated, and the extracted fluorescence lifetime is now 4.19 ns with an error of ±0.02 ns, in very good agreement with the expected value for fluorescein at pH=7.4 [4].

VI. CONCLUSION

A fast and efficient correction method to improve the transfer function of a Time to Digital Converter is presented. The approach is based on the measurement of a large number of Poisson process events generated by a simple SPAD lightened by a CW light source. In addition, this characterization process permits the measurement of the TDC transfer function without the need for any expensive delay generator to calibrate the device. The proposed correction is a post process operation, and thus can be implemented for any type of TDC. Its efficiency is demonstrated in a proof of principle TCSPC experiment. The function transfer correction method is simple, fast, efficient, and does not require hardware design changes of the TDC.

REFERENCES

[1] E. Charbon, M. Fishburn, R. Walker, R. Henderson and C. Niclass, "SPAD-based sensors TOF Range-Imaging Cameras", Springer-Verlag, F Remondino and D Stoppa ed. Berlin Heidelberg, 2013, pp 11–38, doi: 10.1007/978-3-642-27523-4_2.

[2] J. Y. Won, S. I. Kwon, H. S. Yoon, G. B. Ko, J. W. Son and J. S. Lee, "Dual-Phase Tapped-Delay-Line Time-to-Digital Converter With On-the-Fly Calibration Implemented in 40 nm FPGA," in *IEEE Transactions on Biomedical Circuits and Systems*, vol. 10, no. 1, pp. 231-242, 2016. doi: 10.1109/TBCAS.2015.2389227

[3] M. Fishburn, L. H. Menninga, C. Favi and E. Charbon, "A 19.6 ps, FPGA-Based TDC With Multiple Channels for Open Source Applications," in *IEEE Transactions on Nuclear Science*, vol. 60, no. 3, pp. 2203-2208, June 2013.doi: 10.1109/TNS.2013.2241789

[4] Jérémie Léonard, Norbert Dumas, Jean-Pascal Caussé, Sacha Maillot,Naya Giannakopoulou, Sophie Barrea and Wilfried Uhring, "High-throughput time-correlated single photon counting", in *Lab Chip*, 2014, 14, 4338, August 2014, DOI: 10.1039/c4lc00780h

[5] Foudil Dadouche, Timothé Turko, Wilfried Uhring, Imane Malass, Jérémy Bartringer, Jean-Pierre Le Normand, "Design Methodology of TDC on Low Cost FPGA Targets," in *Sensors & Transducers Journal*, vol 193, no. 10, pp 123-134, October 2015

[6] W. Uhring, V. Zint, J. Bartringer, "A low-cost high-repetition-rate picosecond laser diode pulse generator," Photonics Europe Proc. of SPIE, Vol. 5452, 2004. 545038, doi:10.1117/12.545038.

On the Singular Steady-State Output in Discrete-Time Linear Systems

Manuel D. Ortigueira*
* CTS-UNINOVA and Department of Electrical Engineering of
Faculty of Sciences and Technology of Universidade Nova de Lisboa
2829-516 Caparica,Portugal
Email: mdo@fct.unl.pt

Abstract—**The paper deals with discrete-time systems defined by difference equations whose transfer functions may have poles on the unit circle. Contrarily to the regular cases the eigenfunctions of these systems are no longer the exponentials. It is shown that if the input is a product of a falling factorial by an exponential the output is a linear combination of this kind of functions. In particular, the very useful and well-known ARIMA case is studied and exemplified.**

Keywords–ordinary difference equations; constant coefficient; particular solution; eigenfunction; transfer function; singular difference equation

I. Introduction

The constant coefficient ordinary difference equations have a long tradition in applied sciences and have a large amount of enginnering applications, mainly in Signal Processing [1], [3], [4], [10] where they are referred as ARMA (Autoregresive Moving Average) models. In these fields the difference equations are written in the general format

$$\sum_{k=0}^{N} a_k y(n-k) = \sum_{k=0}^{M} b_k x(n-k) \tag{1}$$

wkere $n, M, N \in \mathbf{Z}$ and the coefficients $a_k,\ k = 0, 1, \ldots, N$ and $b_k,\ k = 0, 1, \ldots, M$ are real constants. Although we could consider fractional delays as in [5], we will not do it here.
In the regular case the response of these systems to a sinusoid is also a sinusoid with the same frequency [9], [10] which leads to introduce the frequency response that is another way of describing the system. In a general formulation we can say that the exponentials $\beta^n,\ n \in \mathbf{Z}\, \beta \in \mathbf{C}$ are the eigenfunctions of these systems.
The situation is not so simple in the singular case that we will study in this paper. However and as we will show the role of the exponentials is played by functions defined as the product of a falling factorial by an exponential. Let $(n)_k = n(n-1)(n-2)\ldots(n-k+1)$ be the Pochammer symbol for the falling factorial. We will assume that the input, $x(n)$, is the product of a falling factorial and an exponential defined on $\mathbf{Z}$:

$$x(n) = (n)_K \beta^n \tag{2}$$

where β is any complex number. This function does not have either Z transform or Fourier transform [10]. As we will show, these functions are not eigenfunctions, but we can state: when the input of the system is a function of the type (2) the output is a linear combination of several similar functions. This statement is valid for any regular or irregular system although we will pay a special attention to the irregular cases, mainly the Autoregresive Integrated Moving Average (ARIMA) models. So the frequency responses of these systems loose the normal interpretation. This problem was never considered with generality.
The procedure presented here is formally similar to the one followed in [6]–[8] for dealing with systems defined by differential equations.
We will start by introducing the eigenfunctions of difference equations and compute the corresponding eigenvalues. These are used to obtain the particular solutions we are looking for. Several examples are presented to illustrate the behaviour of the approach.
The objective of this paper is the study of singular cases corresponding to the situations where the transfer function becomes infinite; such situations are treated with all the generality. The important ARIMA model is a particular case with a pole at 1. We will show how to compute the output for these cases.
The paper outline is as follows. In section II, we will introduce the exponentials as eigenfunctions of the ARMA systems. The generalisation for the input as in (2) is done in section III. The singular cases are treated in section IV where the particular ARIMA. At last, we will present some conclusions.

II. The exponentials as eigenfunctions

The discrete convolution is defined by:

$$x(n) * y(n) = \sum_{k=-\infty}^{\infty} x(k) y(n-k), \quad n \in \mathbf{Z} \tag{3}$$

This operation has several interesting properties, but we will study only those interesting for the development we intend to do.

1) Let the Kronecker delta be defined by

$$\delta(n) = \begin{cases} 1 & \text{for } n = 0 \\ 0 & \text{for } n \neq 0 \end{cases} \tag{4}$$

As it is easy to verify, this function is the neutral element of the convolution

$$x(n) = \delta(n) * x(n)$$

2) The convolution is commutative
In fact

$$x(n) * y(n) = y(n) * x(n)$$

as it is easily verified with the substitution $m = n - k$ in (3).

3) A shift in one factor produces the same shift in the convolution. Let $z(n) = x(n) * y(n)$. Then

$$x(n - n_0) * y(n) = z(n - n_0)$$

and using the commutativity

$$y(n-n_0)*x(n) = x(n-n_0)*y(n)$$

For proof we start from (3)

$$x(n-n_0)*y(n) = \sum_{k=-\infty}^{\infty} x(k-n_0)y(n-k)$$

and substitute m for $k-n_0$ to get

$$x(n-n_0)*y(n) = \sum_{m=-\infty}^{\infty} x(m)y(n-n_0-k)$$

With these properties at hand we return to our objective of computing the eigenfunction for equation (1).
Consider a particular input $x(n) = \delta(n)$ and let the corresponding solution be $h(n)$ that we will call Impulse Response. So, this is the solution of

$$\sum_{k=0}^{N} a_k h(n-k) = \sum_{k=0}^{M} b_k \delta(n-k) \tag{5}$$

Now convolve both sides in (5) with $x(n)$.

$$\sum_{k=0}^{N} a_k h(n-k)*x(n) = \sum_{k=0}^{M} b_k \delta(n-k)*x(n)$$

Using the above properties of the convolution we can write

$$\sum_{k=0}^{N} a_k \left[h(n-k)*x(n)\right] = \sum_{k=0}^{M} b_k x(n-k)$$

A comparison of this equation with (1) allows us to conclude that its solution is given by

$$y(n) = h(n)*x(n) \tag{6}$$

This means that the solution of (1) is the convolution of $x(n)$ with the impulse response.

Theorem 2.1: - The particular solution of the difference equation (1) when $x(n) = z^n$, $z \in \mathbf{C}$, $n \in \mathbf{Z}$ is given by

$$y(n) = H(z)z^n \tag{7}$$

provided that $H(z)$ exists.
This theorem shows that the exponentials are the eigenfunctions of the constant coefficient ordinary difference equations.

Proof: Insert $x(n) = z^n$ into (6) and use (3) to get

$$y(n) = \sum_{k=-\infty}^{\infty} h(k)z^{n-k} = \sum_{k=-\infty}^{\infty} h(k)z^{-k}z^n$$

with

$$H(z) = \sum_{k=-\infty}^{\infty} h(k)z^{-k} \tag{8}$$

we obtain (7). $H(z)$ is called *Transfer Function* of the system defined by the difference equation (1) and is the Z transform of the impulse response. ■

Inserting (7) into (1) we conclude immediately that

$$H(z) = \frac{B(z)}{A(z)} = \frac{\sum\limits_{k=0}^{M} b_k z^{-k}}{\sum\limits_{k=0}^{N} a_k z^{-k}} \tag{9}$$

In the following we will consider that the *characteristic polynomial* in the denominator is not zero for the particular value of z at hand. Later we will consider the cases where the characteristic polynomial is zero (z is a pole).

Example 1

Let $x(n) = 2^n$ and consider the equation

$$y(n) = x(n) + x(n-1)$$

We have $H(z) = 1 + z^{-1}$. So the particular solution is given by $y(n) = H(2)2^n = \frac{3}{2}.2^n$ Let now $x(n) = (-1)^n$. We have $y(n) = H(-1)(-1)^n \equiv 0$

Example 2

Consider the difference equation

$$y(n)+y(n-1)-4y(n-2)+2y(n-3) = x(n)+2x(n-1)$$

Let $x(n) = (1/2)^n$. The solution is given by:

$$y(n) = \frac{1+2(1/2)^{-1}}{1+(1/2)^{-1}-4(1/2)^{-2}+2(1/2)^{-3}}(1/2)^n = \frac{5}{3}(1/2)^n$$

The sinusoidal case: – In a particular setting, put $z = e^{i\omega_0}$. We obain immediately

$$y(n) = H(e^{i\omega_0})e^{i\omega_0 n}$$

Example 3

Consider the difference equation

$$y(n) + y(n-1) - 4y(n-2) + y(n-3) = x(n)$$

Let $x(n) = e^{i\frac{\pi}{2}n}$. The solution is given by:

$$y(n) = \frac{1}{1+i^{-1}-4i^{-2}+i^{-3}}e^{i\frac{\pi}{2}n} = \frac{1}{5}e^{i\frac{\pi}{2}n}$$

This is very interesting since it allows us to compute easily the solution when $x(n) = \cos(\omega_o t)$ or $x(n) = \sin(\omega_o t)$. Consider the first case; the second is similar. We have

$$x(n) = \cos(\omega_o t) = \frac{1}{2}e^{i\omega_o n} + \frac{1}{2}e^{-i\omega_o n}$$

that leads to

$$y(n) = H(e^{i\omega_0})\frac{1}{2}e^{i\omega_o n} + H(e^{-i\omega_0})\frac{1}{2}e^{-i\omega_o n}$$

The function $H(e^{i\omega}) = \left|H(e^{i\omega})\right| e^{i\varphi(e^{i\omega})}$ is called *frequency response* in engineering applications. The function $\left|H(e^{i\omega})\right|$ is the *amplitude spectrum* and is an even function, while $\varphi(e^{i\omega})$ is the *phase spectrum* and is an odd function, if the coefficients in (1) are real.

Theorem 2.2: - The particular solution of the difference equation (1) when $x(n) = \cos(\omega_o n)$ is given by

$$y(n) = \left|H(e^{i\omega_o})\right| \cos\left[\omega_o n + \varphi(e^{i\omega_o})\right] \tag{10}$$

Proof: According to what we said above, $|H(e^{-i\omega})| = |H(e^{i\omega})|$ and $\varphi(e^{-i\omega}) = -\varphi(e^{i\omega})$ which leads to

$$y(n) = |H(e^{i\omega_0})| \frac{1}{2} \left[e^{i\omega_0 n} e^{i\varphi(e^{i\omega})} + e^{-i\omega_0 n} e^{-i\varphi(e^{i\omega})} \right]$$

that leads immediately to the result. ∎

It is important to remark that when $H(e^{i\omega_0}) = 0$, $y(n)$ is identically null. This is the reason why we call *filters* the systems described by linear difference equations. This theorem states clearly the importance of the frequency response of a system.

Example 4

Consider again the above equation, but change the second member:

$$y(n) + y(n-1) - 4y(n-2) + y(n-3) = 3x(n) - 4x(n-1)$$

and assume that $x(n) = \sin\left(\frac{\pi}{2} n\right)$. Then

$$H(z) = \frac{3 - 4z^{-1}}{1 + z^{-1} - 4e^{-2} + z^{-3}}$$

and

$$y(n) = \frac{1}{2i} \frac{3 - 4e^{-i\pi/2}}{1 + e^{-i\pi/2} - 4e^{-i\pi} + e^{-i3\pi/2}} e^{i\frac{\pi}{2}n} - \frac{1}{2i} \frac{3 - 4e^{i\pi/2}}{1 + e^{i\pi/2} - 4e^{i\pi} + e^{3\pi/2}} e^{-i\frac{\pi}{2}n}$$

leading to

$$y(n) = \sin\left(\frac{\pi}{2} n + \varphi\right)$$

with $\varphi = \arctan(4/3)$

III. Functions Equal to the Product of a Falling Factorial by an Exponential

To go further we are going to consider the case $x(n) = (n)_K \beta^n$, $n \in \mathbf{Z}, K \in \mathbf{N}_0$. Although not so important as the previous case, it constitutes a simple generalization that is interesting from analytical point of view. It is not difficult to see that we can write $x(n) = \beta^K \lim_{z \to \beta} \frac{d^K}{dz^K} z^n$. Return to (6) and particularise for our case to obtain:

$$y(n) = \sum_{k=-\infty}^{\infty} h(k)(n-k)_K z^{n-k} = \sum_{k=-\infty}^{\infty} h(k) \frac{d^K}{dz^K} z^{n-k}$$

For z in the region of convergence of the Z transform the series converges uniformly and we can commute the derivative and summation operations. This procedure leads to the next theorem.

Theorem 3.1: - The particular solution of the difference equation (1) when $x(n) = (n)_K \beta^n$ is given by

$$y(n) = \beta^K \lim_{z \to \beta} \frac{d^K [H(z) z^n]}{dz^K} \tag{11}$$

Using the Leibniz rule we can obtain another expression for $y(n)$ stated in as follows.

Theorem 3.2: - The particular solution of the difference equation (1) when $x(n) = (n)_K \beta^n$ is given by:

$$y(n) = \sum_{j=0}^{K} \binom{K}{j} H^{(j)}(\beta)(n)_{K-j} \beta^n \tag{12}$$

provided that β is not a pole of the transfer function.

In particular, when $x(n) = (n)_K$ the solution is given by:

$$y(n) = \sum_{j=0}^{K} \binom{K}{j} H^{(j)}(1)(n)_{K-j} \tag{13}$$

For $K = 0$, $x(n) = 1$ and $y(n) = H(1)$.

Example 5

Return back to the above example $y(n) + y(n-1) - 4y(n-2) + y(n-3) = 3x(n) - 4x(n-1)$ and put $x(n) = n$. We obtain immediately

$$y(n) = \sum_{j=0}^{1} \binom{1}{j} H^{(j)}(1)(n)_{1-j}$$

As $H(z) = \frac{3-4z^{-1}}{1+z^{-1}-4e^{-2}+z^{-3}}$, $H(1) = 1$ and $H'(1) = 0$ the solution is

$$y(n) = n$$

IV. The Singular Case - ARIMA

Consider now the situation where the *characteristic polynomial* in the denominator has an mth order root for $z = \beta$. To look for a solution assume that $x(n) = w(n)\beta^n$ and

$$y(n) = v(n).\beta^n \tag{14}$$

Insert $x(n)$ and $y(n)$ into (1) to obtain a new equation

$$\sum_{k=0}^{N} a_k \beta^{-k} v(n-k) = \sum_{k=0}^{M} b_k \beta^{-k} w(n-k) \tag{15}$$

with transfer function $H(\beta z)$. In fact we moved the root of $A(z)$ from $z = \beta$ to $z = 1$. This means that we have a mth order pole at $z = 1$. We can say that we transformed the singular system into an ARIMA system that appears frequently in enonometric studies. In terms of the variable n we have a mth order differentiation at the output. This is equivalent to do an anti-difference on the input. Now perform a new substitution $u(n) = D^m v(n)$ where D means the differencing operation $Dv(n) = v(n) - v(n-1)$ to obtain

$$\sum_{k=0}^{N-m} \bar{a}_k u(n-k) = \sum_{k=0}^{M} \bar{b}_k w(n-k) \tag{16}$$

where $\bar{a}_k$, $k = 0, 1, \ldots, N-m$ are the coefficients of the new characteristic polynomial $\bar{A}(z) = \frac{A(\beta z)}{(1-z^{-1})^m}$ and numerator polynomial $\bar{B}(z) = B(\beta z)$.

For the particular case we are interested in, $w(n) = (n)_K$ we can use (13). Let D^{-1} represent the anti-difference – $D^{-1}Df(n) = DD^{-1}f(n) = f(n)$ – essentially the mth order primitive without primitivation constants. So $v(n) = D^{-m}u(n)$, allowing to obtain the following result.

Theorem 4.1: - The particular solution of the difference equation (1) when $x(n) = (n)_K \beta^n$ with $A(\beta) = 0$ is given by

$$y(n) = \beta^n D^{-m} \left[\sum_{j=0}^{K} \binom{K}{j} \bar{H}^{(j)}(1)(n)_{K-j} \right] \quad (17)$$

with

$$\bar{H}(z) = \frac{\bar{B}(z)}{\bar{A}(z)} = \frac{(1-z^{-1})^m B(\beta z)}{A(\beta z)}$$

It is not difficult to show that (17) can be written as

$$y(n) = \beta^n \left[\sum_{j=0}^{K} \binom{K}{j} \bar{H}^{(j)}(1) \frac{(K-j)!}{(K+m-j)!} (n)_{K+m-j} \right] \quad (18)$$

where we used the following recursively obtained result

$$D^{-m}(n)_K = \frac{K!}{(K+m)!}(n)_{K+m} \quad (19)$$

If $K = 0$ (pure exponential input), we obtain:

$$y(n) = \beta^n \bar{H}(1) \frac{1}{m!}(n)_m \quad (20)$$

If we make $\beta = e^{i\omega_0 n}$ we are led to conclude that the response of the ARIMA model to a pure sinusoid is never a pure sinusoid: the amplitude increases with time. This is the reason why this model is used for modeling non-stationary situations.

Example 6

Consider the following equation with $x(n) = n(-1)^n$

$$y(n) - y(n-1) - 4y(n-2) - 2y(n-3) = x(n)$$

The point $z = -1$ is a pole of the transfer function, $A(-1) = 0$, of order $m = 1$. On the other hand, $\bar{H}(z) = \frac{1+z^{-1}}{1-z^{-1}-4z^{-2}-2z^{-3}} = \frac{1}{1-2z^{-1}-2z^{-2}}$ and $\bar{H}'(z) = -\frac{-2z^{-2}-4z^{-3}}{(1-2z^{-1}-2z^{-2})^2}$, leading to $\bar{H}(-1) = 1$ and $\bar{H}'(-1) = 2$. The solution is $y(n) = [1/2(n)_2 + 2n]\,(-1)^n$.

Example 7

Consider the following ARIMA equation with $x(n) = 1$

$$y(n) - 2y(n-1) + 3y(n-2) - 2y(n-3) = x(n)$$

The point $z = 1$ is a pole of the transfer function, $A(1) = 0$, of order $m = 1$. On the other hand,

$$\bar{H}(z) = \frac{1}{1 - z^{-1} + 2z^{-2}}$$

leading to $\bar{H}(1) = 1/2$. The solution is $y(n) = n/2$.

Example 8

The oscillator is a very interesting system that can be defined by the equation

$$y(n) - 2\cos(\omega_0)y(n-1) + y(n-2) = x(n) - \cos(\omega_0)x(n-1)$$

Now, let $x(n) = e^{i\omega_0 n}$. The system has two simple ($m = 1$) poles at $e^{\pm i\omega_0 n}$. So, $\bar{H}(e^{i\omega_0}) = 1/2$ and the output is easily obtained

$$y(n) = \frac{1}{2} n e^{i\omega_0 n}$$

As we said above, it is a non-stationary model.

V. Conclusions

The singular steady-state output in discrete-time linear systems was studied using an eigenfunction approach to the computation of the steady-state output. Products of falling factorial and exponentials were used as inputs and the corresponding outputs computed in a simple way. Some examples were used to illustrate the procedure, in particular the ARIMA case was considered.
This formulation can be used to study the autocorrelation function of the output when the input is a stationary stochastic process.

Acknowledgments

This work was partially supported by National Funds through the Foundation for Science and Technology of Portugal under project PEst–UID/EEA/00066/2013

References

[1] S. Elaydi, "An introduction to difference equations," Springer, 3rd edition, 2000.

[2] J. Jia and T. Sogabe "On particular solution of ordinary differential equations with constant coefficients," Applied Mathematics and Computation 219 (2013) 6761-6767.

[3] C. Jordan, "Calculus of Finite Differences," Chelsea Publishing Company, New York, 1950, second edition.

[4] H. Levy and F. Lessman, "Finite difference equations," Dover, 1992.

[5] M.D., Ortigueira, "Introduction to Fractional Signal Processing. Part 2: Discrete-Time Systems," IEE Proc. on Vision, Image and Signal Processing, No.1, pp.71-78, 2000.

[6] M. D. Ortigueira, "A simple approach to the particular solution of constant coefficient ordinary differential equations," Applied Mathematics and Computation 232 (2014) 254-260.

[7] M. D. Ortigueira, "On the particular solution of constant coefficient fractional differential equations," Applied Mathematics and Computation, 245:255 - 260, 2014.

[8] Ortigueira, M.D., Coito, F.V., and Trujillo, J.J., "Discrete-time differential systems," Signal Processing 107 (2015) 198-217

[9] J. G. Proakis and D. G. Manolakis, "Digital signal processing: Principles, algorithms, and applications," Prentice Hall, 2007.

[10] M. J. Roberts, "Signals and systems: Analysis using transform methods and Matlab," McGraw-Hill, 2003.

An Improved Empirical Mode Decomposition for Long Signals

J.L. Sánchez*, Manuel D. Ortigueira†, Raul T. Rato‡, and Juan J. Trujillo§
* Departamento de Ingeniería Informática y de sistemas
Universidad de La Laguna 38271 La Laguna, Tenerife, Spain
Email: jsanrosa@ull.edu.es
† UNINOVA and DEE of Faculdade de Ciências e Tecnologia da UNL
Caparica,Portugal
Email: mdo@fct.unl.pt
‡ UNINOVA and Escola Superior de Tecnologia do Instituto Politecnico de Setubal,
2910-761 Setubal, Portugal
Email: raul.rato@estsetubal.ips.pt
§ Departamento de Análisis Matemático,
Universidad de La Laguna 38271 La Laguna, Tenerife, Spain
Email:jtrujill@ullmat.es

***Abstract*—The analysis of long signals is relevant in many fields, as biomedical signal analysis. In this paper, a revision of the Empirical Mode Decomposition (EMD), from the application point of view, is done. The increase in number of Intrinsic Mode Functions (IMF) and computational time in long signals are the main problems that have been faced in this work. A solution based on a sliding window is proposed. An adaptive process is used to calculate the size of the sliding Windows. As a result, the effectiveness of the proposed algorithm increases with the length of the signal. Two examples are introduced to illustrate both problems mentioned above.**

Keywords–Empirical mode decomposition; Intrinsic mode function; long signals

I. INTRODUCTION

The Empirical Mode Decomposition (EMD), as was proposed initially by Huang et al [1] is a signal decomposition algorithm based on a successive removal of elemental signals: the Intrinsic Mode Functions (IMF). These are continuous functions such that at any point, the mean value of the envelope defined by the local maxima and the envelope defined by the local minima is zero. They are obtained through an iterative procedure called sifting that is a way of removing the dissymmetry between the upper and lower envelopes in order to transform the original signal into an amplitude modulated (AM) signal. Moreover, as the instantaneous frequency can change from instant to instant, it can be said that each IMF is a simultaneously amplitude and frequency modulated signal (AM/FM). So, the EMD is nothing else than a decomposition into a set of AM/FM modulated signals [2]–[5].

It must be emphasized that EMD is merely a computational algorithm that expresses a given signal as a sum of simpler components. It can not be said that the obtained components are true parts of the signal at hand.

The original algorithm had some implicit difficulties [3], [6]: extrema location, the end effect and the stopping criterion are critical. Some solutions were proposed in [3] and implemented in an algorithm that can be found at [7]. The location and amplitude of the extrema were estimated using a parabolic interpolation. To render less severe the end effect, the maxima and the minima were extrapolated by both sides. A new stopping criterion in the sifting procedure by introducing two resolution factors was defined.

In the last years, several modifications have been proposed to increase the performances of EMD, [8]–[16], [18], [19]. It is important to question if the introduced complexity compensates the quality increase. In this work, it will be preserved the simplicity of the original algorithm while it is increased the reliability and applicability of the decomposition.

In practical applications, there are several tradeoffs among resolution, signal length, the number of IMFs and running time. In fact, an increase in signal length produces two unwanted side-effects. On the one hand, it leads generally to a corresponding increase in the number of IMFs. Consequently, the running time may become so high, that the algorithm will be useless. The increase in the number of IMFs is a very important drawback because it may originate "false" components that are added to one IMF and subtracted to another one or appear isolated. So, in general, there are no guarantees to have IMFs that are really present in the original signal. On the other hand analyzing long signals with EMD is time-consuming or even impossible in a reasonable time [20] due to the fact, that spline interpolation of a large number of points takes a lot of computer resources. In applications to long signals [17], [21] the number of components and the running time would be so high that the algorithm would be almost useless. This problem was recently considered in [20] where the need of a more efficient and faster algorithm to deal with long signals was stated.

The algorithm described in [3] (and other similar EMD algorithms) is not prepared to deal with long signals as it uses only one window with the length of the signal. In section III it is shown the increase in processing time with increasing lengths. In some applications like EEG or ECG procesing we may have to process signals with lengths above 10^6. The processing time makes the existing algorithms almost useless. This suggests it is important to have an algorithm with the same characteristics but faster. In order to reach such goal, a sliding window EMD is proposed where consecutive windows overlap over a pre-specified amount. While [20] proposes to obtain a full EMD at every window, this approach can cause errors when dealing with signals that have fast changes in their

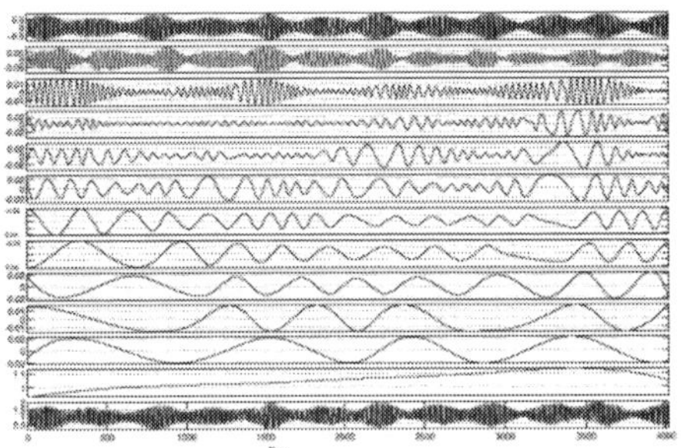

Figure 1. EMD of a tidal signal (in the last strip).

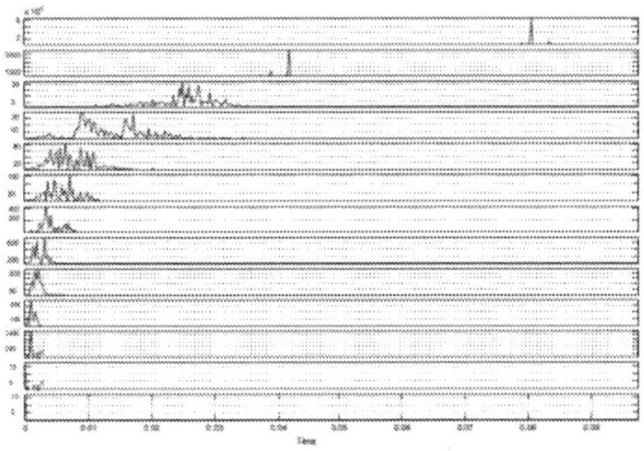

Figure 2. EMD of a tidal signal (in the last strip).

frequency composition. In such case, it could be impossible to obtain a decomposition with the same number of IMF's in all the segments. Our solution follows a different approach. Each IMF is calculated in sliding windows to ensure the number of obtained IMF's components is the same for the whole length of the signal. While [20] proposes to increase the size of the sliding window by a fixed quantity, here it is proposed to duplicate the size of the window when necessary. In that manner, fewer steps are involved for very long signals. Such implies that the length of the signal must be a power of two of the initial window size. Finally, a sliding window algorithm has an overload in the computation of the EMD for signals with a small number of samples. So, the minimum window size must have a lower threshold, corresponding to the length for which the sliding window EMD is slower than the whole length EMD. All these factors together led to an adaptive algorithm. Both, the length of the sliding windows and the length of the overlapping region depends on the length of the whole signal. Also, the overlapping region is tapered to improve the juction between adjacent windows.

The paper outlines as follows. In Section II, some reflections about the EMD are done. In Section III a new method, to analyse long signals, based on a sliding window is proposed. In section IV some illustrating results of the new method are presented. An application to the fan heater example and a comparison with the method in [3] is presented.

II. Some reflections about EMD

It is important to refer the usefulness of EMD in practical applications. A large number of papers published in the last years confirm the affirmation. One of the most important advantages of EMD is the ability to decompose a complex signal into a finite set of narrowband signals without introducing any particular constraint on its characteristics. This makes easier the spectral estimation and creation of simple models.

- Meaning of the IMFs
  In general, it is not possible to establish any special connection between a given IMF and the structure (eventually tied with the underlying physics) of the original signal. This does not mean that it can not be done in some particular situations, as in the case illustrated in Figure 1 where a tidal signal and its EMD are shown.

  A close look seems to point out that the most important IMFs are the two upper ones. The Fourier transform confirms such assumption since the peak frequencies of such IMFs correspond to the frequencies of the main components in the tidal signal: the positions of the Moon and the Sun relative to Earth and the Earth's rotation. The first has a period of about 12 hours and 25 minutes and the second has a period of 24 hours.

  These are clearly identified in the pictures. Even with a careful study it would be more difficult to give some meaning to some of the other components.

- The existence of false components in the IMF's.
  The above example calls the attention to the existence of false components. This can be seen, for instance, in doing a comparison of strips 3 and 4 in Figure 2 where a very similar spectra can be observed. This is a consequence of the numerical errors in sifting: one component is added in one IMF and subtracted in another one.

- The number of IMFs depends on the length of the signal.
  In fact, the number of components increases with the length of the signal. This may be an unwanted feature of the algorithm that is connected with the false component generation. On the other hand, this brings another drawback: the increase in the time required to do the decomposition.

An example

In a search for long range processes, an experiment with the electric circuit of a heater fan was carried out. The signal was sampled during two hours with a sampling interval of 10 ms. With it, the EMD for increasing length segments, using the algorithm described in [3], is computed and the results for 2 different resolutions (45 and 50) are shown in Table 1. Computations were carried out on a PC using MatLab. It is possible to get some decrease in the computational time by implementing the algorithm with a high-level language like *C#* .

It can be concluded that the main drawbacks of EMD are the false components and the large computational time when the signal is long. In the following, we will propose a solution for the second problem that alleviates the first.

TABLE I. IMFs AND COMPUTATIONAL TIME FOR A HEATER FAN SIGNAL

Resol	length	IMFs	time (seconds)
45	11400	14	28
45	27600	15	41
45	114000	18	363
45	340800	20	1057
45	691800	22	3075
50	11400	13	29
50	27600	16	69
50	114000	19	602
50	340800	22	1774
50	691800	22	5195

III. Decomposing long signals

As referred above, the objective of this paper is to propose an algorithm that can be used with long signals with significative reduction in the processing time and eventually in the number of IMFs.

A. The problem

Let $x(t)$ be a given signal to be decomposed by EMD. As referred above the number of IMFs is not known in advance and normally grows up with increasing the length of $x(t)$. This increments the computational burden, leading in some situations to very large computational times making the algorithm useless unless suitable actions are developed – see Table 1. One obvious procedure is to cut the signal into segments. However, this can lead to poor results due to the following

- Different number of IMFs from segment to segment;
- The end effects introduce discontinuities at the junction points.
- Reduced number of extremes leading to poor envelopes.

In [20], there is an attempt to overcome these problems by applying the traditional EMD algorithm to segments of the signal with a fixed number of IMFs. Although this algorithm reduces the computational time, it does not perform a complete true EMD.

In this paper, an algorithm suitable for obtaining the IMFs of very long signals is presented. This situation is very common in mechanical, electrical, and biomedical signal processing [22].

B. The solution

As it has been indicated one of the drawbacks in analyzing long signals is the computational load. The spline interpolation of a large number of points takes a lot of computer resources [20].

For this reason, the use of the sliding window EMD is proposed. The underlying idea to all the algorithms that use sliding windows is to use a divide and conquer strategy. The computation time for spline interpolation is dramatically reduced using smaller segments. However, due to the above referred constraints, too short segments can not be used. It must be taken into account that a sliding window algorithm with few points in each window has an overload due to the repetition of the interpolation. Depending on the features of the computer system used, there exist a threshold below which the classic algorithm is faster than the sliding window method. So, using short windows will result in an increase of the running time. The initial window length is calculated taking into account two factors: The first is that the signal length must be a power of two of the initial window size. The second is the threshold mentioned above. This threshold is set by the user as it depends on its computer system features.

The main idea of the algorithm is to apply the EMD sifting segment to segment to obtain only one IMF at a time. This procedure is done along the whole signal. This ensures that a real EMD is obtained. A pseudocode of our algorithm is:

Input
  $Filename$
  $StartingSample$
  $SignalLength$
$Resolution(dB)$
$OverlapPercentage$
$MinWindowSize$
$MinOscStop$
$MinOscEndStop$
START
  $OptimumSizeWindow = f(SignalLength)$
  $OverlapPoints = f(MinWindowSize$
$, OverlapPercentage)$
  $OSC \leftarrow Inf$
$MINOSC \leftarrow MinOscStop$
WHILE $(OSC > MinOsc)$
  IF $windowsize < Length$

$MINOSC = MinOscEndStop$

$SWEMD(1 : Length, L0, MINOSC)$
  ELSE
$MINOSC = MinOscEndStop$
$EMD(L, MINOSC)$

Figure 3. Adaptative Sliding Window EMD

For a general formulation consider a signal of length L. Select the segment length N and the overlapping M points.

1) Determine the starting window size, the number of samples in the overlap region, and the number of residual samples that do not fit in an integer number of windows.
2) Start a loop to obtain the whole set of IMF.
   a) Start a loop to obtain an IMF on a sliding window basis.
   b) The first window size determines the number of iterations of the sifting process for the rest of the IMF. The stopping criteria for a given IMF is the resolution in dB as proposed in [3].
   c) The process stops when the last segment is processed and the whole IMF is obtained
   d) Continue obtaining IMF's until the stopping criteria for small windows is reached and duplicate the window size.
3) Once the window size equals the whole length, the process continues with a fixed size until the number

of obtained extrema is less or equal than two.

4) Obtain the residual of the decomposition to have the whole EMD decomposition.

The main part of the algorithm is the outer While loop. It controls the stopping criteria for the EMD. The user must select how many oscillations are allowed in the last stage of the actual level. Once it is reached, the window size is duplicated. The process enlarges the size of the window adaptatively as it is needed to analyze components with bigger wavelengths. Moreover, enlarging the window size allow a better interpolation between distant extrema.

Each IMF is calculated with a sliding window if the window size is smaller than the whole signal length. This situation is evaluated in the first part of the IF statement. The situation in which there is only one window for the whole signal is evaluated in the ELSE part.

Segments must be tapered applying a complementary symmetrical window to avoid discontinuities at the boundaries. The windows are overlapped on both sides. A complementary symmetrical window is applied to consecutive segments. The function $\cos^2(\frac{\pi}{2M}n)$, $n = 0, 1, \ldots, M$, is used on the right of the segment and $\sin^2(\frac{\pi}{2M}n)$, $n = 0, 1, \ldots, M$, on the left. Of course, other windows can be used, as it is the case of the triangular.

To implement this process it is necessary to take into account the following observations:

1) The starting window size is correlated to the length of the signal to be analyzed. A simple possibility is making the starting segment a sub-power 2^{-k} of the signal length. On the other hand, a minimal window size must be imposed to avoid an excessive number of partitions. In this manner, the last window will cover the whole length signal. It must be taken into account that, dividing the signal length by powers of two can lead to a non-integer size of the starting window; the integer part of the quotient is used. So the signal length is covered by an integer number of windows and a residual. Depending on its size this residual can be assigned to the last window, enlarging its size or constitute a new window, usually with different size to the previous one.
2) Regarding the criterion to determine when to enlarge the signal, it must be taken into account the fact that the minimum frequency to be analyzed depends on the window size (as it has been indicated before). As the sifting process requires oscillatory signals, it must be ensured that the window contains at least a minimum number of periods that can be selected by the user. The criterion of duplicating the window size when the number of extrema in the previous IMF is lower than a user selected threshold was adopted.
3) Concerning the overlap region, it must be taken into account that it is necessary to reduce the undesirable end effects. Extrapolation is not used, since there are enough number of samples outside the actual segment. That implies that overlapping consecutive windows solve both, boundary and end effects.

IV. Illustrating Results

In the following, the behavior of the algorithm is illustrated. Firstly, the fan signal mentioned above is decomposed using the algorithm in [3]. The result is shown in Figure 4. Secondly, the same signal is decomposed using the method proposed here. The result can be observed in Figure 5. A comparison of the computation time and the number of IMF obtained with both algorithms is presented in Table 2.

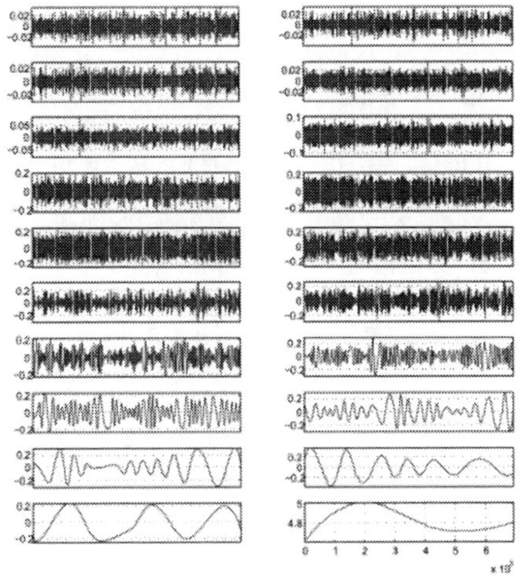

Figure 4. EMD using algorithm of [3]

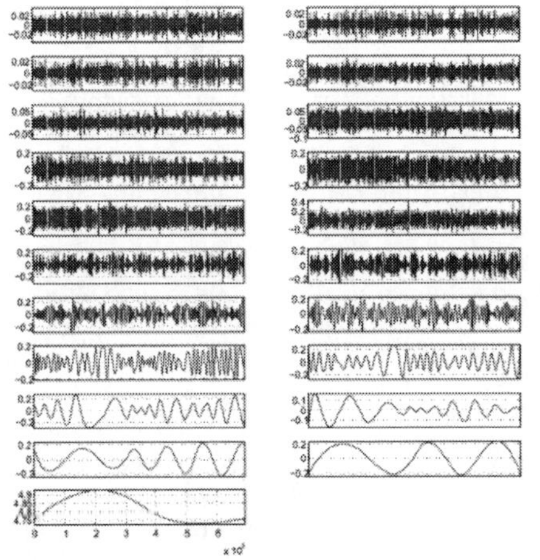

Figure 5. EMD using algorithm proposed here.

TABLE II. TIME COMPARISON BETWEEN BOTH ALGORITHMS FOR A HEATER FAN SIGNAL

Resol	length	IMFs	time EMD as in [3]	IMFs	time new EMD
45	11400	14	28	14	17
45	27600	15	41	14	37
45	114000	18	363	16	159
45	340800	20	1057	19	452
45	691800	22	3075	20	923
50	11400	13	29	12	23
50	27600	16	69	15	50
50	114000	19	602	18	217
50	340800	22	1774	20	669
50	691800	22	5195	21	1414

While for 11,400 samples the sliding window computation time is 79% of the EMD calculated as in [3], for 691,800 samples the computation time is only 27%. That is due to the fact that the window size increases by powers of two, which results in smaller running times for very long signals. So, the effectiveness of the proposed adaptive sliding window algorithm increases with the length of the signal. Despite of the fact of using many windows for the calculation, the obtained IMF's show a high quality as no discontinuities can be observed in the last IMF's for a signal with more than 600,000 samples.

It must be taken into account that any error in a given IMF is propagated to the rest of the decomposition. As subsequent components have smaller amplitudes, the errors have greater importance. Our algorithm has shown a good behavior as it can be observed in 5. That is due to the fact that averaging the overlapped region between two consecutive windows smooths the result. As the number of samples in the overlapping region is based on a fixed percentage of the window size, the number of samples change with the window size.

V. CONCLUSIONS

The Empirical Mode Decomposition is a technique to decompose any signal into a finite set of narrowband components, the Intrinsic Mode Functions. The number of components and computational time increase dramatically when the length of the signal becomes large. Proposals for solving this problem had been done, but without the required quality. A modified sifting algorithm to deal with long signals was proposed here. It is based on computing every IMF using a sliding window. The algorithm is adaptive as both, the length of the sliding windows and the overlapping region depends on the signal to be analized. The change on the length of the sliding window by powers of two has two positive consequences. On one hand, the final window will cover the whole length of the signal in a few steps. On the other hand, the effectiveness of the proposed method increases with the length of the signal. The application of our method confirms the affirmation.

ACKNOWLEDGMENTS

This work was partially funded by National Funds through the Foundation for Science and Technology of Portugal, under the project PEst-UID/EEA/00066/2013 and by project MTM2013-417 from Government of Spain.

REFERENCES

[1] Norden E. Huang et al., "The empirical mode decomposition and Hilbert spectrum for nonlinear and non-stationary time series analysis." Proceedings of the Royal Society of London A, vol. 454, issue 1971, 1998, pp. 903–995.

[2] S. Peng, X. Hu, and W. L. Hwang, "Multicomponent am-fm signal separation and demodulation with null space pursuit." Signal, Image and Video Processing, vol. 7, issue 6, 2013, pp. 1093-1102.

[3] R. T. Rato, M. D. Ortigueira and A. G. Batista, "On the HHT, its problems, and some solutions." Mechanical Systems and Signal Processing, vol. 22, issue 6, 2008, pp. 1374–1394,

[4] R. T. Rato, M. D. Ortigueira and A. G. Batista, "The EMD and its use to identify system modes." In Proceedings of the International Workshop on New Trends in Science and Technology [CD-ROM], Nov. 03-04, 2008, Ankara, Turkey.

[5] M. K. Hasan, K. M. S. Apu and M. K. I. Molla, "A robust method for parameter estimation of ar systems using empirical mode decomposition." Signal, Image and Video Processing, vol. 4, issue 4, 2010, pp. 451-461.

[6] P. C. Chu, C. W. Fan and N. Huang, "Compact empirical mode decomposition: an algorithm to reduce mode mixing, end effect, and detrend uncertainty." Advances in Adaptive Data Analysis, vol. 4, issue 3, 2012, pp. 1250017 (18 pages).

[7] M. Ortigueira, "Empirical Mode Decomposition [online]" Available: http://www.mathworks.com/matlabcentral/fileexchange/21409-empirical-mode-decomposition. [Accessed: 18- Apr- 2016]

[8] K. M. Chang and S. H. Liu, "Gaussian noise filtering from ECG by wiener filter and ensemble empirical mode decomposition." Journal of Signal Processing Systems, Special Issue "Signal Processing Circuits and Systems for Bio-Signals", vol. 64, issue 2, 2011, pp. 249-264.

[9] M. A. Colominas, G. Schlotthauer and M. E. Torres, "Improved complete ensemble EMD: A suitable tool for biomedical signal processing." Biomedical Signal Processing and Control, vol. 14, 2014, pp. 19–29.

[10] M. Feldman, "Analytical basics of the EMD: Two harmonics decomposition." Mechanical Systems and Signal Processing, vol. 23, issue 7, 2009, pp. 2059-2071.

[11] X. Guanlei, W. Xiaotong, X. Xiaogang and Z. Lijia, "Improved EMD for the analysis of fm signals." Mechanical Systems and Signal Processing, vol. 33, 2012, pp. 181–196.

[12] H. Jiang, C. Li and H. Li, "An improved EEMD with multiwavelet packet for rotating machinery multi-fault diagnosis." Mechanical Systems and Signal Processing, vol. 36, issue 2, 2013, pp. 225-239.

[13] Z. K. Peng, P. W. Tse and F. L. Chu, "An improved Hilbert-Huang transform and its application in vibration signal analysis." Journal of Sound and Vibration, vol. 286, issues 1-2, 2005, pp. 187–205

[14] N. U. Rehman, C. Park, N. E. Huang and D. P. Mandic, "Emd via MEMD: Multivariate noise-aided computation of standard EMD." Advances in Adaptive Data Analysis, vol. 5, issue 2, 2013, pp. 1350007 (25 pages).

[15] P. Singh, P. K. Srivastava, R. K. Patney, S. D. Joshi and K. Saha, "Nonpolynomial spline based empirical mode decomposition." In International Conference on Signal Processing and Communication (ICSC), Noida, India, December 2013, pp. 435–440, IEEE.

[16] Y. Yang, J. Deng and D. Kang, "An improved empirical mode decomposition by using dyadic masking signals." Signal, Image and Video Processing, vol. 9, issue 6, 2013, pp. 1259–1263.

[17] F. Ebrahimia, S. K. Setarehdana and H. Nazeranb, "Automatic sleep staging by simultaneous analysis of ECG and respiratory signals in long epochs." Biomedical Signal Processing and Control, vol. 18, 2015, pp. 69–79.

[18] X. D. Yu, M. Y. Zhang, M. Q. Zhu, K. H. Xu and Q. C. Xiang, "An improved extension method of EMD based on svrm." Applied Mechanics and Materials, vol. 543-547, 2014, pp. 2697–2701.

[19] A. Eftekhar, C. Toumazou, E. M. Drakakis, "Empirical mode decomposition: Real-time implementation and applications." Journal of Signal Processing Systems, vol. 73, issue 1, 2013, pp. 43–58.

[20] P. Stepien, "Sliding window empirical mode decomposition – its performance and quality." EPJ Nonlinear Biomedical Physics, vol. 2, issue 1, 2014, pp. 2–14.

[21] Md. A. Kabir and C. Shahnaz, "Denoising of ECG signals based on noise reduction algorithms in EMD and wavelet domains." Biomedical Signal Processing and Control, vol. 7, issue 5, 2012, pp. 481–489.

[22] M. P. Pierzchalski, R. A. Stepien, P. Stepien, "New nonlinear methods of heart rate variability analysis in diagnostics of atrial fibrillation." International Journal of Biology and Biomedical Engineering, vol. 5, issue 4, pp. 201-208, 2011.